Lesson Planner

PRENTICE HALL

AMERICA
PATHWAYS TO THE PRESENT

PEARSON
Prentice
Hall

Needham, Massachusetts
Upper Saddle River, New Jersey

Pearson Prentice Hall™ is a trademark of Pearson Education, Inc.
Pearson® is a registered trademark of Pearson plc.
Prentice Hall® is a registered trademark of Pearson Education, Inc.

ISBN 0-13-128381-2

3 4 5 6 7 8 9 10   08 07 06

Table of Contents

Chapter 1   The Atlantic World

Chapter 2   European Colonization of the Americas

Chapter 3   Growth of the American Colonies

Chapter 4   The Road to Independence

Chapter 5   The Constitution of the United States

Chapter 6   The Origins of American Politics

Chapter 7   Life in the New Nation

Chapter 8   The Growth of a National Economy

Chapter 9   Religion and Reform

Chapter 10   The Coming of the Civil War

Chapter 11   The Civil War

Chapter 12   Reconstruction

Table of Contents *(continued)*

Table of Contents (*continued*)

How To Use This Guide

This book will simplify lesson planning for you. A summary of the Teacher's Edition lesson plan as well as targeted resources for each portion of the lesson are presented here on a single page. The lesson planner has been designed to ensure that you will be able to

- Pace your teaching to cover everything in the course.
- Select resources to meet diverse student needs.
- Monitor student progress at regular intervals.

In addition to the year-long pacing charts in the front of this book, you will find a reproducible lesson plan for each section in your textbook. Just fill in your name and class day, check the resources you will use, and add in the homework you plan to assign.

Lesson Objectives

Key Vocabulary

Summary of each step of the lesson

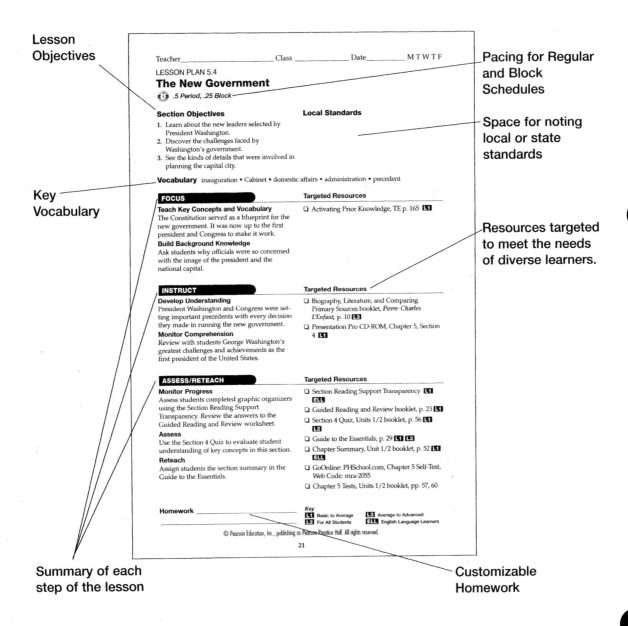

Pacing for Regular and Block Schedules

Space for noting local or state standards

Resources targeted to meet the needs of diverse learners.

Customizable Homework

PACING GUIDE CHART

The following pacing chart shows how the chapters and sections of *America: Pathways to the Present* can be adapted to fit your specific course focus and time constraints.

Chapter/Section	U.S. History Survey	Block Schedule
Chapter 1: The Atlantic World, to 1600		
Section 1 The Native American World	1	.5
Section 2 The European World	1	.5
Section 3 The World of the West Africans	.5	.25
Section 4 The Atlantic World Is Born	1	.5
Chapter 2: European Colonization of the Americas, 1492–1752		
Section 1 Spanish Explorers and Colonies	1	.5
Section 2 Jamestown	1	.5
Section 3 The New England Colonies	1	.5
Section 4 The Middle and Southern Colonies	.5	.25
Chapter 3: Growth of the American Colonies, 1689–1754		
Section 1 An Empire and Its Colonies	1	.5
Section 2 Life in Colonial America	1	.5
Section 3 African Americans in the Colonies	1	.5
Section 4 Emerging Tensions	.5	.25
Chapter 4: The Road to Independence, 1753–1783		
Section 1 The French and Indian War	.5	.25
Section 2 Issues Behind the Revolution	1	.5
Section 3 Ideas Behind the Revolution	.5	.25
Section 4 Fighting for Independence	1	.5
Section 5 Winning Independence	.5	.25
Chapter 5: The Constitution of the United States, 1776–1800		
Section 1 Government by the States	1	.5
Section 2 The Constitutional Convention	1	.5
Section 3 Ratifying the Constitution	1	.5
Section 4 The New Government	.5	.25
Chapter 6: The Origins of American Politics, 1789–1820		
Section 1 Liberty Versus Order in the 1790s	1	.5
Section 2 The Election of 1800	1	.5
Section 3 The Jefferson Administration	1	.5
Section 4 Native American Resistance	.5	.25
Section 5 The War of 1812	1	.5
Chapter 7: Life in the New Nation, 1783–1830		
Section 1 Cultural, Social, and Religious Life	1	.5
Section 2 Trails to the West	1	.5
Section 3 The Great Plains and the Southwest	1	.5
Chapter 8: The Growth of a National Economy, 1790–1850		
Section 1 Inventions and Innovations	1	.5
Section 2 The Northern Section	.5	.25
Section 3 The Southern Section	.5	.25
Section 4 The Growth of Nationalism	1	.5
Section 5 The Age of Jackson	1	.5
Chapter 9: Religion and Reform, 1800–1850		
Section 1 Reforming Society	1	.5
Section 2 The Antislavery Movement	1	.5
Section 3 The Movement for Women's Rights	1	.5
Section 4 Growing Divisions	.5	.25

PACING GUIDE CHART

Chapter/Section	U.S. History Survey	Block Schedule
Chapter 10: The Coming of the Civil War, 1848–1861		
Section 1 Two Nations	.5	.25
Section 2 The Mexican War and Slavery Extension	.5	.25
Section 3 New Political Parties	1	.5
Section 4 The System Fails	1	.5
Section 5 A Nation Divided Against Itself	.5	.25
Chapter 11: The Civil War, 1861–1865		
Section 1 From Bull Run to Antietam	1	.5
Section 2 Life Behind the Lines	1	.5
Section 3 The Tide of War Turns	1	.5
Section 4 Devastation and New Freedom	1	.5
Chapter 12: Reconstruction, 1865–1877		
Section 1 Presidential Reconstruction	1	.5
Section 2 Congressional Reconstruction	1	.5
Section 3 Birth of the "New South"	.5	.25
Section 4 The End of Reconstruction	.5	.25
Chapter 13: The Expansion of American Industry, 1850–1900		
Section 1 A Technological Revolution	1	.5
Section 2 The Growth of Big Business	1	.5
Section 3 Industrialization and Workers	.5	.25
Section 4 The Great Strikes	1	.5
Chapter 14: Looking to the West, 1860–1900		
Section 1 Moving West	.5	.25
Section 2 Conflict with Native Americans	1	.5
Section 3 Mining, Ranching, and Farming	1	.5
Section 4 Populism	1	.5
Chapter 15: Politics, Immigration, and Urban Life, 1870–1915		
Section 1 Politics in the Gilded Age	1	.5
Section 2 People on the Move	1	.5
Section 3 The Challenge of the Cities	1	.5
Section 4 Ideas for Reform	.5	.25
Chapter 16: Life at the Turn of the Twentieth Century, 1870–1915		
Section 1 The Expansion of Education	1	.5
Section 2 New Forms of Entertainment	.5	.25
Section 3 The World of Jim Crow	.5	.25
Section 4 The Changing Roles of Women	.5	.25
Chapter 17: Becoming a World Power, 1890–1915		
Section 1 The Pressure to Expand	.5	.25
Section 2 The Spanish-American War	1	.5
Section 3 A New Foreign Policy	1	.5
Section 4 Debating America's New Role	.5	.25
Chapter 18: The Progressive Reform Era, 1890–1920		
Section 1 The Origins of Progressivism	.5	.25
Section 2 Progressive Legislation	1	.5
Section 3 Progressivism Under Taft and Wilson	1	.5
Section 4 Suffrage at Last	.5	.25
Chapter 19: The World War I Era, 1914–1920		
Section 1 The Road to War	.5	.25
Section 2 The United States Declares War	.5	.25
Section 3 Americans on the European Front	1	.5
Section 4 Americans on the Home Front	.5	.25
Section 5 Global Peacemaker	1	.5

PACING GUIDE CHART

Chapter/Section	U.S. History Survey	Block Schedule
Chapter 20: Postwar Social Change, 1920–1929		
Section 1 Society in the 1920s	1	.5
Section 2 Mass Media and the Jazz Age	1	.5
Section 3 Cultural Conflicts	1	.5
Chapter 21: Politics and Prosperity, 1920–1929		
Section 1 A Republican Decade	1	.5
Section 2 A Business Boom	1	.5
Section 3 The Economy in the Late 1920s	.5	.25
Chapter 22: Crash and Depression, 1929–1933		
Section 1 The Stock Market Crash	.5	.25
Section 2 Social Effects of the Depression	1	.5
Section 3 Surviving the Great Depression	.5	.25
Section 4 The Election of 1932	1	.5
Chapter 23: The New Deal, 1933–1941		
Section 1 Forging a New Deal	1	.5
Section 2 The New Deal's Critics	1	.5
Section 3 Last Days of the New Deal	1	.5
Chapter 24: World War II: The Road to War, 1931–1941		
Section 1 Rise of Dictators	1	.5
Section 2 Europe Goes to War	.5	.25
Section 3 Japan Builds an Empire	.5	.25
Section 4 From Isolationism to War	.5	.25
Chapter 25: World War II: Americans at War, 1941–1945		
Section 1 Mobilization	1	.5
Section 2 Retaking Europe	1	.5
Section 3 The Holocaust	.5	.25
Section 4 The War in the Pacific	1	.5
Section 5 The Social Impact of the War	1	.5
Chapter 26: The Cold War, 1945–1960		
Section 1 Origins of the Cold War	1	.5
Section 2 The Cold War Heats Up	1	.5
Section 3 The Korean War	.5	.25
Section 4 The Continuing Cold War	.5	.25
Chapter 27: The Postwar Years at Home, 1945–1960		
Section 1 The Postwar Economy	1	5
Section 2 The Mood of the 1950s	.5	.25
Section 0 Domestic Politics and Policy	1	.5
Chapter 28: The Civil Rights Movement, 1950–1968		
Section 1 Demands for Civil Rights	1	.5
Section 2 Leaders and Strategies	.5	.25
Section 3 The Struggle Intensifies	1	.5
Section 4 The Political Response	1	.5
Section 5 The Movement Takes a New Turn	1	.5
Chapter 29: The Kennedy and Johnson Years, 1961–1969		
Section 1 The New Frontier	1	.5
Section 2 The Great Society	1	.5
Section 3 Foreign Policy in the Early 1960s	1	.5
Chapter 30: An Era of Activism, 1960–1975		
Section 1 The Women's Movement	1	.5
Section 2 Ethnic Minorities Seek Equality	1	.5
Section 3 The Counterculture	.5	.25
Section 4 The Environmental and Consumer Movements	.5	.25

PACING GUIDE CHART

Chapter/Section	U.S. History Survey	Block Schedule
Chapter 31: The Vietnam War, 1954–1975		
Section 1 The War Unfolds	.5	.25
Section 2 Fighting the War	1	.5
Section 3 Political Divisions	1	.5
Section 4 The End of the War	1	.5
Chapter 32: Nixon, Ford, Carter, 1969–1981		
Section 1 Nixon's Domestic Policy	1	.5
Section 2 Nixon's Foreign Policy	1	.5
Section 3 The Watergate Scandal	1	.5
Section 4 The Ford Administration	.5	.25
Section 5 The Carter Administration	1	.5
Chapter 33: The Conservative Revolution, 1980–1992		
Section 1 Roots of the New Conservatism	.5	.25
Section 2 The Reagan Revolution	1	.5
Section 3 Reagan's Second Term	1	.5
Section 4 The George H. W. Bush Presidency	1	.5
Chapter 34: Entering a New Era, 1992 to the Present		
Section 1 Politics in Recent Years	.5	.25
Section 2 The United States in a New World	1	.5
Section 3 Americans in the New Millennium	1	.5

LESSON PLAN 1.1

The Native American World

⏱ *1 Period, .5 Block*

Section Objectives

Local Standards

1. Find out how the Americas were settled and how the settlers adapted to the environment of North America.
2. Learn about the customs and beliefs shared by early Native Americans.
3. Discover how trade and beliefs about land affected Native American economies.

Vocabulary migration • kinship • clan • oral history • barter

---

FOCUS

Targeted Resources

Teach Key Concepts and Vocabulary
Ask students to compare images of Native American culture they are familiar with from museums, movies, and popular art.

Build Background Knowledge
Despite vast regional differences, Native American groups maintained shared customs and beliefs.

❏ Activating Prior Knowledge, TE p. 4 **L1**
❏ Color Transparencies, Historical Maps, A1; Time Lines, C1; **L2**
❏ Historical Outline Map Book, *Hunters Reach America*, p. 1; *Native American Cultures*, p.4 **L1**
❏ Sounds of an Era Audio CD, *The Iroquois Constitution*, Ely S. Parker **L3**

INSTRUCT

Targeted Resources

Develop Understanding
Discuss how the environment influenced the lifestyles of the various groups that inhabited North America.

Monitor Comprehension
Ask students to name some of the ways Native Americans were able to maintain shared customs and beliefs.

❏ Learning Styles Lesson Plan booklet, p. 4 **L2**
❏ Presentation Pro CD-ROM, Chapter 1, Section 1 **L1**
❏ Prentice Hall U.S. History Video Collection, Vol. 1, *Three Worlds Meet* **L2**

ASSESS/RETEACH

Targeted Resources

Monitor Progress
Assess students completed graphic organizers using the Section Reading Support Transparency. Review the answers to the Guided Reading and Review worksheet.

Assess
Use the Section 1 Quiz to evaluate student understanding of key concepts in this section.

Reteach
Assign students the section summary in the Guide to the Essentials.

❏ Section Reading Support Transparency **L1** **ELL**
❏ Guided Reading and Review booklet, p. 3 **L1**
❏ Section 1 Quiz, Units 1/2 booklet, p. 4 **L1** **L2**
❏ Guide to the Essentials, p. 6 **L1** **L2**
❏ Guided Reading Audiotapes **ELL**
❏ Student Edition on Audio CD **ELL**

Homework _____

_____

Key

L1 Basic to Average   **L3** Average to Advanced
L2 For All Students   **ELL** English Language Learners

LESSON PLAN 1.2

The European World

🕐 *1 Period, .5 Block*

Section Objectives

1. Find out what life was like in Europe during the Early Middle Ages.
2. See what changes took place during the Late Middle Ages.
3. Read to find out about the Renaissance.

Local Standards

Vocabulary Middle Ages • feudalism • Crusades • middle class • monarch • Magna Carta • Renaissance • Reformation

---

FOCUS

Teach Key Concepts and Vocabulary
Ask students what skills and qualities Europeans needed to possess in order to begin exploring the world.

Build Background Knowledge
Explain how the European worldview changed during the Renaissance.

Targeted Resources

❏ Activating Prior Knowledge, TE p. 10 **L1**

INSTRUCT

Develop Understanding
What role did the Renaissance play in the development of trans-Atlantic trade?

Monitor Comprehension
Ask students to list some of the most important changes that took place in Europe during the transition between the Middle Ages and the Renaissance.

Targeted Resources

❏ Learning with Documents booklet, Magna Carta, p. 79; *Mapmakers*, p. 40 **L3**

❏ Biography, Literature, and Comparing Primary Sources booklet, *The Koran*, p. 40 **L3**

❏ Presentation Pro CD-ROM, Chapter 1, Section 2 **L1**

❏ Exploring Primary Sources in U.S. History CD-ROM, *Magna Carta* **L3**

ASSESS/RETEACH

Monitor Progress
Assess students' completed graphic organizers using the Section Reading Support Transparency. Review the answers to the Guided Reading and Review worksheet.

Assess
Use the Section 2 Quiz to evaluate student understanding of key concepts in this section.

Reteach
Assign students the section summary in the Guide to the Essentials.

Targeted Resources

❏ Section Reading Support Transparency **L1** **ELL**

❏ Guided Reading and Review booklet, p. 4 **L1**

❏ Section 2 Quiz, Units 1/2 booklet, p. 5 **L1** **L2**

❏ Guide to the Essentials, p. 6 **L1** **L2**

❏ Social Studies Skills Tutor CD-ROM **L1**

❏ Guided Reading Audiotapes **ELL**

❏ Student Edition on Audio CD **ELL**

Homework _____

_____

Key
L1 Basic to Average **L3** Average to Advanced
L2 For All Students **ELL** English Language Learners

LESSON PLAN 1.3

The World of West Africans

⏱ .5 Period, .25 Block

Section Objectives	**Local Standards**

1. Learn how West Africans and Europeans first met.
2. Find out some key features of early West African cultures.
3. See how a trading relationship developed between Europe and the kingdoms of West Africa.
4. Discover the role of slavery in African society.

Vocabulary savanna • lineage • scarce

FOCUS

Teach Key Concepts and Vocabulary
Explain that the first interactions between European and African cultures came in the 1400s along the coast of West Africa.

Build Background Knowledge
In the 1400s, prosperous kingdoms with complex cultures could be found throughout West Africa.

Targeted Resources
❑ Activating Prior Knowledge, TE p. 17 **L1**
❑ Historical Outline Map Book, *The World*, p. 71 **L1**
❑ Sounds of an Era Audio CD, *Olaudah Equiano* **L3**

INSTRUCT

Develop Understanding
Discuss the extent of West African trade routes with students.

Monitor Comprehension
Ask students how West African kingdoms were different from European kingdoms. How were they similar?

Targeted Resources
❑ Presentation Pro CD-ROM, Chapter 1, Section 3 **L1**

ASSESS/RETEACH

Monitor Progress
Assess students' completed graphic organizers using the Section Reading Support Transparency. Review the answers to the Guided Reading and Review worksheet.

Assess
Use the Section 3 Quiz to evaluate student understanding of key concepts in this section.

Reteach
Assign students the section summary in the Guide to the Essentials.

Targeted Resources
❑ Section Reading Support Transparency **L1** **ELL**
❑ Guided Reading and Review booklet, p. 5 **L1**
❑ Section 3 Quiz, Units 1/2 booklet, p. 6 **L1** **L2**
❑ Guide to the Essentials, p. 7 **L1** **L2**
❑ Social Studies Skills Tutor CD-ROM **L1**
❑ Guided Reading Audiotapes **ELL**
❑ Student Edition on Audio CD **ELL**

Homework _____

_____

Key
L1 Basic to Average   **L3** Average to Advanced
L2 For All Students   **ELL** English Language Learners

Teacher_____ Class _____ Date_____ M T W T F

LESSON PLAN 1.4
The Atlantic World Is Born
1 Period, .5 Block

Section Objectives

1. See what is known about the early life of Christopher Columbus.
2. Find out about events that occurred on Columbus' expeditions.
3. Learn about the debate concerning the impact of Columbus' voyages.

Local Standards

Vocabulary Columbian Exchange • Treaty of Tordesillas • plantation • cash crop

FOCUS

Teach Key Concepts and Vocabulary
The interaction of Native Americans, Europeans, and Africans following Columbus's trans-Atlantic voyage created what is termed the Atlantic World.

Build Background Knowledge
Point out that the Europeans seemed to dominate the Atlantic World.

Targeted Resources

❏ Activating Prior Knowledge, TE p. 22 **L1**
❏ Historical Outline Map Book, *To India by Sea*, p. 6; *Columbus Reaches America*, p. 7 **L1**
❏ Sounds of an Era Audio CD, *Letter to the Spanish Crown, Christopher Columbus* **L3**

INSTRUCT

Develop Understanding
Centuries of interaction between Native Americans, Europeans, and Africans brought great changes to each culture.

Monitor Comprehension
Have students list the ways in which Columbus's voyages changed the histories of the Americas, Europe, and Africa.

Targeted Resources

❏ Skills for Life booklet p. 3 **L1**
❏ Learning Styles Lesson Plan booklet, p. 5 **L2**
❏ Learning with Documents booklet, *Europeans Encounter Native Americans*, p. 6 **L3**
❏ Biography, Literature, and Comparing Primary Sources booklet, *Isabella I, Queen of Castille*, p. 6; *On Celebrating Columbus Day*, pp. 97-98 **L3**
❏ Exploring Primary Sources in U.S. History CD-ROM, *The Log of Christopher Columbus* **L3**
❏ American Heritage, My Brush with History, *The Search for Riches in North America*, Student Edition pp. 32–33, Videotape

ASSESS/RETEACH

Monitor Progress
Assess students completed graphic organizers using the Section Reading Support Transparency.

Assess
Use the Section 4 Quiz to evaluate student understanding of key concepts in this section.

Reteach
Assign students the Guide to the Essentials.

Homework _____

Targeted Resources

❏ Guided Reading and Review booklet, p. 6 **L1**
❏ Section 4 Quiz, Units 1/2 booklet, p. 7 **L1 L2**
❏ Guide to the Essentials, p. 8 **L1 L2**
❏ Summary, Units 1/2 booklet, p. 3 **L1 ELL**
❏ GoOnline: PHSchool.com, Chapter 1 Self-Test, Web Code: mra-1015
❏ Chapter 1 Tests, Unit 1/2 booklet, pp. 8, 11

Key
L1 Basic to Average   **L3** Average to Advanced
L2 For All Students   **ELL** English Language Learners

LESSON PLAN 2.1
Spanish Explorers and Colonies
🕐 *1 Period, .5 Block*

Section Objectives   ## Local Standards

1. Find out how the Spanish built an empire in the Americas.
2. See why the Spanish pushed for settlement in regions of North America.
3. Learn how Native Americans resisted the Spanish.

Vocabulary colony • hidalgo • isthmus • conquistador • *encomienda* system • mestizo • presidio • mission • congregación • Pueblo Revolt of 1680

FOCUS

Teach Key Concepts and Vocabulary
Ask students to state some of the goals of the Spanish exploration in North America.

Build Background Knowledge
Explain to students how European Christians' belief in their duty to spread their own religion throughout the world affected their dealings with Native Americans.

Targeted Resources
❑ Activating Prior Knowledge, TE p. 36 **L1**
❑ Color Transparencies, Historical Maps, A2 **L2**
❑ Historical Outline Map Book, *Spanish Explorers in North America*, p. 9; *Spain and Portugal in the Americas*, p. 11 **L1**

INSTRUCT

Develop Understanding
Discuss with students the Spanish pattern of conquest. How did this pattern repeat itself in the Americas?

Monitor Comprehension
Have students sketch maps of North, Central, and South America. Ask them to indicate the areas explored by the Spanish, including key settlements.

Targeted Resources
❑ Biography, Literature, and Comparing Primary Sources booklet, *Bartolomé de Las Casas*, p. 7 **L3**
❑ Presentation Pro CD-ROM, Chapter 2, Section 1 **L1**

ASSESS/RETEACH

Monitor Progress
Assess students' completed graphic organizers using the Section Reading Support Transparency. Review the answers to the Guided Reading and Review worksheet.

Assess
Use the Section 1 Quiz to evaluate student understanding of key concepts in this section.

Reteach
Assign students the section summary in the Guide to the Essentials.

Targeted Resources
❑ Section Reading Support Transparency **L1**
❑ Guided Reading and Review booklet, p. 7 **L1**
❑ Section 1 Quiz, Units 1/2 booklet, p. 15 **L1** **L2**
❑ Guide to the Essentials, p. 10 **L1** **L2**
❑ Social Studies Skills Tutor CD-ROM **L1**
❑ Guided Reading Audiotapes **ELL**
❑ Student Edition on Audio CD **ELL**

Homework _____

_____

Key
L1 Basic to Average   **L3** Average to Advanced
L2 For All Students   **ELL** English Language Learners

LESSON PLAN 2.2
Jamestown
⏱ *1 Period, .5 Block*

Section Objectives
1. Discover the goals of England's explorers.
2. Learn about the challenges faced by Jamestown's early settlers.
3. Discover the role of tobacco in Virginia and find out how it contributed to Bacon's Rebellion.
4. See why relations were uneasy between English settlers and Native Americans.

Local Standards

Vocabulary privateer • charter • joint-stock company • royal colony • legislature • House of Burgesses • indentured servant • Bacon's Rebellion

FOCUS

Teach Key Concepts and Vocabulary
Ask students to list the challenges facing the settlers at Jamestown.
Build Background Knowledge
In its early days the Jamestown colony nearly failed, and many of its first settlers died due to hunger and disease.

Targeted Resources
❑ Activating Prior Knowledge, TE p. 42 **L1**
❑ Historical Outline Map Book, *The First English Settlements*, p. 14 **L1**
❑ Sounds of an Era Audio CD, *The First Voyage Made to the Coasts of America*, Roger Barlowe **L3**

INSTRUCT

Develop Understanding
The production of tobacco saved the Jamestown colony from failure. What other problems did it solve? What new problems did it create?
Monitor Comprehension
How might the English colonists have better prepared themselves to settle Jamestown?

Targeted Resources
❑ Learning Styles Lesson Plan booklet, p. 6 **L2**
❑ Learning with Documents booklet, *Cultural Clashes in the Virginia Colony*, p. 7 **L3**
❑ Biography, Literature, and Comparing Primary Sources booklet, *On Life in Jamestown*, pp. 99–100; *The Fate of an Indentured Servant*, p. 41 **L3**
❑ Presentation Pro CD-ROM, **L1**

ASSESS/RETEACH

Monitor Progress
Assess students' completed graphic organizers using the Section Reading Support Transparency. Review the answers to the Guided Reading and Review worksheet.
Assess
Use the Section 2 Quiz to evaluate student understanding of key concepts in this section.
Reteach
Assign students the section summary in the Guide to the Essentials.

Targeted Resources
❑ Section Reading Support Transparency **L1 ELL**
❑ Guided Reading and Review booklet, p. 8 **L1**
❑ Section 2 Quiz, Units 1/2 booklet, p. 16 **L1 L2**
❑ Guide to the Essentials, p. 11 **L1 L2**
❑ Social Studies Skills Tutor CD-ROM **L1**
❑ Guided Reading Audiotapes **ELL**
❑ Student Edition on Audio CD **ELL**

Homework _____

_____

Key
L1 Basic to Average   **L3** Average to Advanced
L2 For All Students   **ELL** English Language Learners

LESSON PLAN 2.3

The New England Colonies

🕐 *1 Period, .5 Block*

Section Objectives

1. Learn about the pattern of French settlement in North America.
2. Discover the goals of the Plymouth and Massachusetts Bay colonies.
3. Understand why there was dissent within the puritan community.
4. See why war broke out between the Indians and the English settlers.

Local Standards

Vocabulary New England Colonies • Puritan • persecute • Pilgrim • Mayflower Compact • Great Migration •religious tolerance •Salem witch trials • sachem • Pequot War • King Philip's War

---

FOCUS

Teach Key Concepts and Vocabulary
Have students list some reasons for expanded colonial settlement in North America by both the English and the French.

Build Background Knowledge
Ask students to compare the French pattern of interaction with Native Americans with the English pattern of interaction with Native Americans.

Targeted Resources

❑ Activating Prior Knowledge, TE p. 49 **L1**
❑ Color Transparencies, Historical Maps, A3 **L2**
❑ Historical Outline Map Book, *Search for a Northwest Passage*, p. 10; *The French Explore North America*, p. 12; *The New England Colonies*, p. 16 **L1**
❑ Sounds of an Era Audio CD, *"A Modell of Christian Charity,"* John Winthrop **L3**

INSTRUCT

Develop Understanding
English settlement provoked resentment in Native Americans in New England, culminating in several wars in the 1600s.

Monitor Comprehension
Have students discuss steps the Puritan settlers might have taken to improve relations with Native Americans.

Targeted Resources

❑ Learning Styles Lesson Plan booklet, p. 7 **L2**
❑ Learning with Documents booklet, *The Mayflower Compact*, p. 75; *A Lasting Stereotype*, p. 41 **L3**
❑ Presentation Pro CD-ROM, Chapter 2, Section 3 **L1**
❑ Exploring Primary Sources in U.S. History CD-ROM, *Mayflower Compact* **L3**

ASSESS/RETEACH

Monitor Progress
Assess students' completed graphic organizers using the Section Reading Support Transparency.

Assess
Use the Section 3 Quiz to evaluate student understanding of key concepts in this section.

Reteach
Assign students the Guide to the Essentials.

Targeted Resources

❑ Section Reading Support Transparency **L1** **ELL**
❑ Guided Reading and Review booklet, p. 9 **L1**
❑ Section 3 Quiz, Units 1/2 booklet, p. 17 **L1 L2**
❑ Guide to the Essentials, p. 12 **L1 L2**
❑ Social Studies Skills Tutor CD-ROM **L1**
❑ Guided Reading Audiotapes **ELL**
❑ Student Edition on Audio CD **ELL**

Homework _____

_____

Key
L1 Basic to Average   **L3** Average to Advanced
L2 For All Students   **ELL** English Language Learners

LESSON PLAN 2.4

The Middle and Southern Colonies

⏱ *.5 Period, .25 Block*

Section Objectives

1. Discover the early history of the Dutch in New York.
2. Find out about the characteristics of the other Middle Colonies.
3. See why people settled in the Southern Colonies.

Local Standards

Vocabulary Middle Colonies • diversity • synagogue • proprietary colony • Quaker • haven • Southern Colonies • trustee

FOCUS

Teach Key Concepts and Vocabulary
Ask students why the Dutch established a colony in what is now New York. How did their beliefs affect the development of the colony?

Build Background Knowledge
Tell students that the colonies south of New England were not dominated by Puritans. Many Middle and Southern Colonies showed religious tolerance.

Targeted Resources

❑ Activating Prior Knowledge, TE p. 59 **L1**
❑ Historical Outline Map Book, *New Netherland and New Sweden*, p. 13; *The Middle Colonies*, p. 17; *The Southern Colonies*, p. 18 **L1**

INSTRUCT

Develop Understanding
Most of the Middle and Southern Colonies were proprietary colonies. The individuals or group that was granted the proprietorship could make the laws.

Monitor Comprehension
Discuss how settlers' philosophies shaped the colonies they established.

Targeted Resources

❑ Skills for Life booklet p. 4 **L1**
❑ Presentation Pro CD-ROM, Chapter 1, Section 4 **L1**

ASSESS/RETEACH

Monitor Progress
Assess students' completed graphic organizers using the Section Reading Support Transparency. Review the answers to the Guided Reading and Review worksheet.

Assess
Use the Section 4 Quiz to evaluate student understanding of key concepts in this section.

Reteach
Assign students the section summary in the Guide to the Essentials.

Targeted Resources

❑ Section Reading Support Transparency **L1 ELL**
❑ Guided Reading and Review booklet, p. 10 **L1**
❑ Section 4 Quiz, Units 1/2 booklet, p. 18 **L1 L2**
❑ Guide to the Essentials, p. 13 **L1 L2**
❑ Chapter Summary, Units 1/2 booklet, p. 14 **L1 ELL**
❑ GoOnline: PHSchool.com, Chapter 1 Self-Test, Web Code: mra-1025
❑ Chapter 2 Tests, Units 1/2 booklet, pp. 19, 22

Homework _____

_____

Key
L1 Basic to Average   **L3** Average to Advanced
L2 For All Students   **ELL** English Language Learners

LESSON PLAN 3.1

An Empire and Its Colonies

⏰ *1 Period, .5 Block*

Section Objectives	Local Standards

Section Objectives

1. Find out how the English Civil War affected the development of the colonies.
2. See how mercantilism influenced England's colonial laws and foreign policy.
3. Learn about Britain's colonial policy in the early 1700s.
4. Discover which farming, trade, and settlement patterns defined the diverse economies of the colonies.

Vocabulary mercantilism • balance of trade • duty • salutary neglect • staple crop • triangular trade

---

FOCUS

Teach Key Concepts and Vocabulary
Why did England purposely neglect its colonies in the late 1600s and early 1700s?

Build Background Knowledge
Explain that the relationship between England and its colonies was generally peaceful but distant during this period. The colonies developed into prosperous but distinct regions.

Targeted Resources

- ❏ Activating Prior Knowledge, TE p. 70 **L1**
- ❏ Color Transparencies, Historical Maps, A4 **L2**
- ❏ Historical Outline Map Book, *The New England Colonies*, p. 16; *The Middle Colonies*, p. 17; *The Southern Colonies*, p. 18; *Major Trade Routes*, p. 19 **L1**

INSTRUCT

Develop Understanding
England used the prosperity of its colonies to accumulate wealth in accordance with the theory of mercantilism. Charles II passed the Navigation Act in order to bring more money to the English treasury.

Monitor Comprehension
Ask students to name some of the ways in which the English colonies prospered. What were some of the causes of this prosperity?

Targeted Resources

- ❏ Skills for Life booklet p. 5 **L1**
- ❏ Presentation Pro CD-ROM, Chapter 3, Section 1 **L1**

ASSESS/RETEACH

Monitor Progress
Assess students completed graphic organizers using the Section Reading Support Transparency.

Assess
Use the Section 1 Quiz to evaluate student understanding of key concepts in this section.

Reteach
Assign students' the Guide to the Essentials.

Homework _____

_____

Targeted Resources

- ❏ Section Reading Support Transparency **L1** **ELL**
- ❏ Guided Reading and Review booklet, p. 11 **L1**
- ❏ Section 1 Quiz, Units 1/2 booklet, p. 26 **L1** **L2**
- ❏ Guide to the Essentials, p. 15 **L1** **L2**

Key
L1 Basic to Average   **L3** Average to Advanced
L2 For All Students   **ELL** English Language Learners

LESSON PLAN 3.2
Life in Colonial America
1 Period, .5 Block

Section Objectives
Local Standards

1. Learn how colonial society was organized.
2. Find out why wealth in land was important.
3. Discover some of the common trades and occupations in the colonies.
4. Read to know more about the rights and responsibilities of colonial women.
5. Understand the nature of work and education in the colonies.

Vocabulary gentry • apprentice • almanac • indigo • self-sufficient

FOCUS
Targeted Resources

Teach Key Concepts and Vocabulary
What aspects of daily life governed the lives of most people in colonial America?

Build Background Knowledge
Explain that colonists created a hierarchical society. Ask students who held power.

❑ Activating Prior Knowledge, TE p. 77 **L1**
❑ Color Transparencies, Historical Maps, A5, A56 **L2**
❑ Sounds of an Era Audio CD, *The Autobiography of Benjamin Franklin* **L3**

INSTRUCT
Targeted Resources

Develop Understanding
Colonial society was unequal. A person's status was evidenced by their work as well as by their gender. Ask students how work in colonial times differed from work today.

Monitor Comprehension
Have students create a hierarchy of colonial society, giving a brief description of each sector.

❑ Learning with Documents booklet, *A Marriage Agreement*, p. 8; *The First American Schoolbook*, p. 42 **L3**
❑ Biography, Literature, and Comparing Primary Sources booklet, *As Poor Richard Says*, p. 42 **L3**
❑ Presentation Pro CD-ROM, Chapter 3, Section 2 **L1**

ASSESS/RETEACH
Targeted Resources

Monitor Progress
Assess students' completed graphic organizers using the Section Reading Support Transparency. Review the answers to the Guided Reading and Review worksheet.

Assess
Use the Section 2 Quiz to evaluate student understanding of key concepts in this section.

Reteach
Assign students the section summary in the Guide to the Essentials.

❑ Section Reading Support Transparency **L1** **ELL**
❑ Guided Reading and Review booklet, p. 12 **L1**
❑ Section 2 Quiz, Units 1/2 booklet, p. 27 **L1** **L2**
❑ Guide to the Essentials, p. 16 **L1** **L2**
❑ Social Studies Skills Tutor CD-ROM **L1**
❑ Guided Reading Audiotapes **ELL**
❑ Student Edition on Audio CD **ELL**

Homework _____
_____

Key
L1 Basic to Average **L3** Average to Advanced
L2 For All Students **ELL** English Language Learners

LESSON PLAN 3.3

African Americans in the Colonies

1 Period, .5 Block

Section Objectives

1. Learn about the Middle Passage.
2. Find out how the experience of slavery differed from colony to colony.
3. See the restrictions faced by free blacks.
4. Discover how laws attempted to control slaves and prevent revolts.

Vocabulary Middle Passage • mutiny • Stono Rebellion

Local Standards

FOCUS

Teach Key Concepts and Vocabulary
Ask students to describe what life was like for African Americans living in the colonies.

Build Background Knowledge
Tell students that, excluding Native Americans, about 20 percent of the people living in colonial America were of African descent.

Targeted Resources
❏ Activating Prior Knowledge, TE p. 83 **L1**
❏ Sounds of an Era Audio CD, *Gullah Storyteller Janie Hunter* **L3**

INSTRUCT

Develop Understanding
Though fewer in number, Africans in the New England and Middle Colonies had more varied occupations than those in the Southern Colonies. Africans enslaved on Southern plantations were able to maintain some of their language and traditions.

Monitor Comprehension
Have students list some of the ways in which slaves contributed to the prosperity of the colonies.

Targeted Resources
❏ Learning Styles Lesson Plan booklet, p. 8 **L2**
❏ Presentation Pro CD-ROM, Chapter 3, Section 3 **L1**
❏ Exploring Primary Sources in U.S. History CD-ROM, *"Swing Low, Sweet Chariot,"* Spiritual **L3**

ASSESS/RETEACH

Monitor Progress
Assess students completed graphic organizers using the Section Reading Support Transparency. Review the answers to the Guided Reading and Review worksheet.

Assess
Use the Section 3 Quiz to evaluate student understanding of key concepts in this section.

Reteach
Assign students the section summary in the Guide to the Essentials.

Targeted Resources
❏ Section Reading Support Transparency **L1** **ELL**
❏ Guided Reading and Review booklet, p. 13 **L1**
❏ Section 3 Quiz, Units 1/2 booklet, p. 28 **L1** **L2**
❏ Guide to the Essentials, p. 17 **L1** **L2**
❏ Social Studies Skills Tutor CD-ROM **L1**
❏ Guided Reading Audiotapes **ELL**
❏ Student Edition on Audio CD **ELL**

Homework _____

Key
L1 Basic to Average   **L3** Average to Advanced
L2 For All Students   **ELL** English Language Learners

LESSON PLAN 3.4

Emerging Tensions

⏱ *.5 Period, .25 Block*

Section Objectives

1. Find out what drove the western expansion of colonial settlement.
2. Learn how Native Americans and the French reacted to the expansion of the colonies.
3. Discover why the Great Awakening both resolved and contributed to religious tensions.

Local Standards

Vocabulary immigrant • migration • Great Awakening • itinerant • dissent

FOCUS

Teach Key Concepts and Vocabulary
How was the revival of religious feeling a challenge to both colonial society and British rule?

Build Background Knowledge
Review with students why the French and Native Americans did not welcome English settlers as they pushed westward.

Targeted Resources
❑ Activating Prior Knowledge, TE p. 89 **L1**
❑ Historical Outline Map Book, *North America in 1753*, p. 20 **L1**
❑ Sounds of an Era Audio CD, *"Sinners in the Hands of an Angry God,"* Jonathan Edwards **L3**

INSTRUCT

Develop Understanding
Expanding British settlement caused tension with Native Americans and French fur trappers. Religious tensions threatened the social order. Preachers of the Great Awakening stressed the importance of figures of authority.

Monitor Comprehension
Ask students what steps the British settlers might have taken to minimize friction with Native Americans.

Targeted Resources
❑ Learning Styles Lesson Plan booklet, p. 9 **L2**
❑ Biography, Literature, and Comparing Primary Sources booklet, *On Expansion into Native American Lands*, pp. 101–102; Jonathan Edwards, p. 8 **L3**
❑ Presentation Pro CD-ROM, Chapter 3, Section 4 **L1**

ASSESS/RETEACH

Monitor Progress
Assess students' completed graphic organizers using the Section Reading Support Transparency. Review the answers to the Guided Reading and Review worksheet.

Assess
Use the Section 4 Quiz to evaluate student understanding of key concepts in this section.

Reteach
Assign students the section summary in the Guide to the Essentials.

Targeted Resources
❑ Section Reading Support Transparency **L1** **ELL**
❑ Guided Reading and Review booklet, p. 14 **L1**
❑ Section 4 Quiz, Units 1/2 booklet, p. 29 **L1** **L2**
❑ Guide to the Essentials, p. 18 **L1** **L2**
❑ Chapter Summary, Units 1/2 booklet, p. 25 **L1** **ELL**
❑ GoOnline: PHSchool.com, Chapter 3 Self-Test, Web Code: mra-1035
❑ Chapter 3 Tests, Units 1/2 booklet, pp. 30, 33

Homework _____

_____

Key
L1 Basic to Average   **L3** Average to Advanced
L2 For All Students   **ELL** English Language Learners

LESSON PLAN 4.1

The French and Indian War

🕐 .5 Period, .25 Block

Section Objectives

1. Learn about the causes of the French and Indian War.
2. Find out how the British won the French and Indian War.
3. See how war weakened the colonists' loyalty to Britain.

Vocabulary French and Indian War • Albany Plan of Union • militia • prime minister • siege • Treaty of Paris (1763)

Local Standards

FOCUS

Teach Key Concepts and Vocabulary
The French and Indian War was a turning point in the relationship between Great Britain and its American colonists.

Build Background Knowledge
Have students recall what they already know about the relationship between the English colonists and Native Americans, and the relationship between the French colonists and Native Americans prior to the French and Indian War.

Targeted Resources
❏ Activating Prior Knowledge, TE p. 104 **L1**
❏ Color Transparencies, Historical Maps, A6 **L2**
❏ Historical Outline Map Book, *The French and Indian War*, p. 21 **L1**

INSTRUCT

Develop Understanding
During the French and Indian War, British colonists discovered their own distinctly American identity.

Monitor Comprehension
What aspects of the French and Indian War caused many colonists to change their view about their relationship with Great Britain?

Targeted Resources
❏ Learning with Documents booklet, *Braddock's Defeat*, p. 9 **L3**
❏ Biography, Literature, and Comparing Primary Sources booklet, *Laying Siege to Quebec*, p. 43 **L3**
❏ Presentation Pro CD-ROM, Chapter 4, Section 1 **L1**
❏ Prentice Hall U.S. History Video Collection, Vol. 4, *The American Revolution* **L2**

ASSESS/RETEACH

Monitor Progress
Assess students' completed graphic organizers using the Section Reading Support Transparency.

Assess
Use the Section 1 Quiz to evaluate student understanding of key concepts in this section.

Reteach
Assign students the Guide to the Essentials.

Targeted Resources
❏ Section Reading Support Transparency **L1** **ELL**
❏ Guided Reading and Review booklet, p. 15 **L1**
❏ Section 1 Quiz, Units 1/2 booklet, p. 41 **L1** **L2**
❏ Guide to the Essentials, p. 20 **L1** **L2**
❏ Guided Reading Audiotapes **ELL**

Homework _____
_____

Key
L1 Basic to Average   **L3** Average to Advanced
L2 For All Students   **ELL** English Language Learners

13

LESSON PLAN 4.2

Issues Behind the Revolution

1 Period, .5 Block

Section Objectives

1. See how and why British policies in the colonies changed after 1763.
2. Learn about the causes and effects of the Stamp Act.
3. Discover how rising tensions in the colonies led to fighting at Lexington and Concord.

Local Standards

Vocabulary Pontiac's Rebellion • Proclamation of 1763 • Stamp Act • boycott • Boston Massacre • First Continental Congress • Battles of Lexington and Concord • Revolutionary War

FOCUS

Teach Key Concepts and Vocabulary
In order to increase tax revenues, Great Britain began to tighten its control over the colonies following the French and Indian War.

Build Background Knowledge
Ask students to recall Great Britain's policy toward its American colonies before the French and Indian War.

Targeted Resources

❏ Activating Prior Knowledge, TE p. 109 **L1**
❏ Color Transparencies, Historical Maps, A60; Time Lines, C2 **L2**
❏ Historical Outline Map Book, *The North America in 1763*, p. 22; *Lexington and Concord*, p. 23; *The Revolutionary War: An Overview*, p. 24 **L1**
❏ Sounds of an Era Audio CD, *Newspaper Account of the Battle of Lexington and Concord* **L3**

INSTRUCT

Develop Understanding
Colonists reacted strongly to increased British control, believing that their rights as British citizens were being violated.

Monitor Comprehension
Have students analyze colonists' protests. Do they think the colonists were justified in their discontent?

Targeted Resources

❏ Skills for Life booklet p. 6 **L1**
❏ Learning with Documents booklet, *Boycotting Tea*, p. 43 **L3**
❏ Presentation Pro CD-ROM, Chapter 4, Section 2 **L1**
❏ Exploring Primary Sources in U.S. History CD-ROM, *The Bloody Massacre, 1770*, **L3**

ASSESS/RETEACH

Monitor Progress
Assess students' completed graphic organizers using the Section Reading Support Transparency.

Assess
Use the Section 2 Quiz to evaluate student understanding of key concepts in this section.

Reteach
Assign students the section summary in the Guide to the Essentials.

Targeted Resources

❏ Section Reading Support Transparency **L1** **ELL**
❏ Guided Reading and Review booklet, p. 16 **L1**
❏ Section 2 Quiz, Units 1/2 booklet, p. 42 **L1** **L2**
❏ Guide to the Essentials, p. 21 **L1** **L2**
❏ Social Studies Skills Tutor CD-ROM **L1**
❏ Guided Reading Audiotapes **ELL**

Homework _____

_____

Key
L1 Basic to Average   **L3** Average to Advanced
L2 For All Students   **ELL** English Language Learners

LESSON PLAN 4.3

Ideas Behind the Revolution

🕐 *.5 Period, .25 Block*

Section Objectives

1. Find out about the importance of Thomas Paine's *Common Sense*.
2. See what ideas and arguments are presented in the Declaration of Independence.
3. Learn more about the advice Abigail Adams gave her husband regarding the Declaration.

Vocabulary *Common Sense* • Second Continental Congress • Olive Branch Petition • Declaration of Independence • Enlightenment • preamble • natural rights • rule of law

Local Standards

FOCUS

Teach Key Concepts and Vocabulary
Ask students why Common Sense was important to the development of democracy.

Build Background Knowledge
New ideas that challenged authority spurred the Revolution as well as the actions of Great Britain.

Targeted Resources

❏ Activating Prior Knowledge, TE p. 118 **L1**
❏ Sounds of an Era Audio CD, *The Declaration of Independence* **L3**

INSTRUCT

Develop Understanding
Ideas such as those put forth by Thomas Paine and Thomas Jefferson fueled the War for Independence and helped create a new society.

Monitor Comprehension
Ask students to explain what role new ideas about equality and self-government played in the American Revolution.

Targeted Resources

❏ Learning Styles Lesson Plan booklet, p. 10 **L2**
❏ Learning with Documents booklet, Patrick Henry, *Speech to the Virginia Provincial Convention*, p. 76 **L3**
❏ Biography, Literature, and Comparing Primary Sources booklet, *On Rule By the People*, p. 103 **L3**
❏ Presentation Pro CD-ROM, Chapter 4, Section 3 **L1**
❏ Exploring Primary Sources in U.S. History CD-ROM, *Common Sense*, Thomas Paine; *The New American Man*, Michel-Guillaume Jean de Crèvecoeur, **L3**

ASSESS/RETEACH

Monitor Progress
Assess students' completed graphic organizers using the Section Reading Support Transparency.

Assess
Use the Section 3 Quiz to evaluate student understanding of key concepts in this section.

Reteach
Assign students the Guide to the Essentials.

Targeted Resources

❏ Section Reading Support Transparency **L1** **ELL**
❏ Guided Reading and Review booklet, p. 17 **L1**
❏ Section 3 Quiz, Units 1/2 booklet, p. 43 **L1** **L2**
❏ Guide to the Essentials, p. 22 **L1** **L2**

Homework _____

_____

Key
L1 Basic to Average   **L3** Average to Advanced
L2 For All Students   **ELL** English Language Learners

LESSON PLAN 4.4

Fighting for Independence

1 Period, .5 Block

Section Objectives

1. Discover what happened during the siege of Boston.
2. Find out about the strengths and weaknesses of the British and American forces.
3. See why the Battle of Saratoga was considered a turning point of the war.

Vocabulary Battle of Bunker Hill • casualty • Loyalist • mercenary • Battle of Trenton • Battle of Saratoga

Local Standards

FOCUS

Teach Key Concepts and Vocabulary
Both the American and British forces had strengths and weaknesses in the War for Independence.

Build Background Knowledge
Read students Thomas Paine's famous words: "These are the times that try men's souls." Ask students why colonists might be conflicted over going to war with Great Britain.

Targeted Resources
❏ Activating Prior Knowledge, TE p. 127 **L1**
❏ Historical Outline Map Book, *The Revolutionary War in the Northeast*, p. 25 **L1**
❏ Sounds of an Era Audio CD, *Sylvanus Woods and Lieutenant Barker on the Revolutionary War* **L3**

INSTRUCT

Develop Understanding
Not all colonists were Patriots. Loyalists continued to support the crown, while others remained neutral. The Battle of Saratoga turned the tide of the war in favor of the Americans.

Monitor Comprehension
Have students create a chart comparing the strengths and weaknesses of the British and American positions in the period 1775–1777.

Targeted Resources
❏ Learning Styles Lesson Plan booklet, p. 11 **L2**
❏ Presentation Pro CD-ROM, Chapter 3, Section 4 **L1**
❏ American Heritage, My Brush with History, *Diary of a Wartime Winter*, Student Edition pp. 140–141, Videotape **L2**

ASSESS/RETEACH

Monitor Progress
Assess students completed graphic organizers using the Section Reading Support Transparency.

Assess
Use the Section 4 Quiz to evaluate student understanding of key concepts in this section.

Reteach
Assign students the Guide to the Essentials.

Targeted Resources
❏ Section Reading Support Transparency **L1 ELL**
❏ Guided Reading and Review booklet, p. 18 **L1**
❏ Section 4 Quiz, Units 1/2 booklet, p. 44 **L1 L2**
❏ Guide to the Essentials, p. 23 **L1 L2**
❏ Guided Reading Audiotapes **ELL**
❏ Student Edition on Audio CD **ELL**

Homework _____

_____

Key
L1 Basic to Average   **L3** Average to Advanced
L2 For All Students   **ELL** English Language Learners

LESSON PLAN 4.5

Winning Independence

.5 Period, .25 Block

Section Objectives

1. Learn about hardships endured by Americans during the war.
2. See how American victories in the West and South led to the end of the war.
3. Discover the impact of the American Revolution.

Local Standards

Vocabulary blockade • profiteering • inflation • Battle of Yorktown • Treaty of Paris (1783) • patriotism

---

FOCUS

Teach Key Concepts and Vocabulary
The War for Independence was a long and costly war.

Build Background Knowledge
Why do you think colonists persevered despite the many disadvantages they faced fighting the War for Independence?

Targeted Resources

❏ Activating Prior Knowledge, TE p. 133 **L1**
❏ Historical Outline Map Book, *The Revolutionary War in the West*, p. 26; *The Revolutionary War in the South*, p. 27; *North America in 1783*, p. 28 **L1**
❏ Sounds of an Era Audio CD, *Champ Clark on Valley Forge* **L3**

INSTRUCT

Develop Understanding
American independence from Britain was won at great cost. Discuss with students the course of the war and why victory was so long in coming.

Monitor Comprehension
Have students explain the importance of British defeats in the West and South to the outcome of the war.

Targeted Resources

❏ Biography, Literature, and Comparing Primary Sources booklet, Deborah Sampson Gannett, p. 9 **L3**
❏ Presentation Pro CD-ROM, Chapter 4, Section 5 **L1**

ASSESS/RETEACH

Monitor Progress
Assess students' completed graphic organizers using the Section Reading Support Transparency. Review the answers to the Guided Reading and Review worksheet.

Assess
Use the Section 5 Quiz to evaluate student understanding of key concepts in this section.

Reteach
Assign students the Guide to the Essentials.

Targeted Resources

❏ Section Reading Support Transparency **L1** **ELL**
❏ Guided Reading and Review booklet, p. 19 **L1**
❏ Section 5 Quiz, Units 1/2 booklet, p. 45 **L1** **L2**
❏ Guide to the Essentials, p. 24 **L1** **L2**
❏ Social Studies Skills Tutor CD-ROM **L1**
❏ Guided Reading Audiotapes **ELL**
❏ Chapter Summary, Units 1/2 booklet, p. 40 **L1** **ELL**
❏ GoOnline: PHSchool.com, Chapter 4 Self-Test, Web Code: mra-2046
❏ Chapter 4 Tests, Units 1/2 booklet, pp. 46, 49

Homework _____

_____

Key
L1 Basic to Average   **L3** Average to Advanced
L2 For All Students   **ELL** English Language Learners

LESSON PLAN 5.1
Government by the States
🕐 *1 Period, .5 Block*

Section Objectives

1. Describe the early government of the United States.
2. State some reasons for opposition to the Articles of Confederation.
3. Learn about the causes and effects of Shays' Rebellion.

Vocabulary Articles of Confederation • legislative branch • executive branch • judicial branch • constitution • democracy • republic • Shays' Rebellion • specie

Local Standards

FOCUS

Teach Key Concepts and Vocabulary
Ask students to describe the role of the Articles of Confederation in the establishment of the United States government.

Build Background Knowledge
Review with students the ideas that fueled the American Revolution.

Targeted Resources

❑ Activating Prior Knowledge, TE p. 144 **L1**

INSTRUCT

Develop Understanding
While many Americans were happy with the weak national government formed under the Articles of Confederation, it was harshly criticized by the Nationalists, who believed the United States would benefit from a strong central government.

Monitor Comprehension
Have students debate the merits of a strong versus weak national government as either a supporter of the Articles of Confederation or a Nationalist.

Targeted Resources

❑ Biography, Literature, and Comparing Primary Sources booklet, *On the United States as an Independent Nation*, p. 105–106 **L3**

❑ Presentation Pro CD-ROM, Chapter 5, Section 1 **L1**

❑ Prentice Hall U.S. History Video Collection, Vol. 5, *A New Nation* **L2**

ASSESS/RETEACH

Monitor Progress
Assess students completed graphic organizers using the Section Reading Support Transparency.

Assess
Use the Section 1 Quiz to evaluate student understanding of key concepts in this section.

Reteach
Assign students the Guide to the Essentials.

Targeted Resources

❑ Section Reading Support Transparency **L1** **ELL**

❑ Guided Reading and Review booklet, p. 20 **L1**

❑ Section 1 Quiz, Units 1/2 booklet, p. 53 **L1 L2**

❑ Guide to the Essentials, p. 26 **L1 L2**

❑ Guided Reading Audiotapes **ELL**

Homework _____

_____

Key
L1 Basic to Average   **L3** Average to Advanced
L2 For All Students   **ELL** English Language Learners

LESSON PLAN 5.2

The Constitutional Convention

🕐 *1 Period, .5 Block*

Section Objectives

1. Find out what the Founding Fathers hoped to achieve as they assembled for the Constitutional Convention.
2. Learn about issues that divided the convention.
3. See what the convention did to reach agreement.
4. Discover qualities that have made the Constitution a lasting document.
5. Realize how the government under the Constitution divides power.

Local Standards

Vocabulary Constitutional Convention • United States Constitution • amend • veto • Great Compromise • Three-Fifths Compromise • federal system of government • separation of powers • checks and balances • electoral college

FOCUS

Teach Key Concepts and Vocabulary
The delegates to the Constitutional Convention debated whether power should rest with the states or with the national government.

Build Background Knowledge
Ask students to recall what they know about the weakness in the Articles of Confederation.

Targeted Resources

❏ Activating Prior Knowledge, TE p. 150 **L1**
❏ Color Transparencies, Historical Maps, A55 **L2**
❏ Sounds of an Era Audio CD, *Benjamin Franklin's Constitutional Convention Speech* **L3**

INSTRUCT

Develop Understanding
The Great Compromise and the Three-Fifths Compromise allowed Constitutional Convention delegates to create a lasting document.

Monitor Comprehension
Have students outline the basic structure of the United States government as set forth by the Constitutional Convention of 1787.

Targeted Resources

❏ Learning Styles Lesson Plan booklet, p. 12 **L2**
❏ Learning with Documents booklet, *Hamilton and Jefferson*, p. 10 **L3**
❏ Biography, Literature, and Comparing Primary Sources booklet, *The Real Character of the Executive*, p. 44 **L3**
❏ Presentation Pro CD-ROM, Chapter 5, Section 2 **L1**

ASSESS/RETEACH

Monitor Progress
Assess students completed graphic organizers using the Section Reading Support Transparency.

Assess
Use the Section 2 Quiz to evaluate student understanding of key concepts in this section.

Reteach
Assign students the Guide to the Essentials.

Targeted Resources

❏ Section Reading Support Transparency **L1** **ELL**
❏ Guided Reading and Review booklet, p. 21 **L1**
❏ Section 2 Quiz, Units 1/2 booklet, p. 54 **L1** **L2**
❏ Guide to the Essentials, p. 27 **L1** **L2**

Homework _____

_____

Key
L1 Basic to Average   **L3** Average to Advanced
L2 For All Students   **ELL** English Language Learners

LESSON PLAN 5.3

Ratifying the Constitution

1 Period, .5 Block

Section Objectives

1. Learn how the position of the Federalists differed from that of the anti-Federalists.
2. See how the Federalists won approval of the Constitution.
3. Find out about arguments for and against a Bill of Rights.

Vocabulary ratify • Federalist • faction • anti-Federalist • Bill of Rights

Local Standards

FOCUS

Teach Key Concepts and Vocabulary
To become law, the Constitution needed to be ratified by 9 of the 13 states.

Build Background Knowledge
Anti-Federalists felt the Constitution betrayed the ideals of the Revolution.

Targeted Resources

❏ Activating Prior Knowledge, TE p. 158 **L1**
❏ Color Transparencies, Historical Maps, A8 **L2**
❏ Sounds of an Era Audio CD, *"Federalist No. 51,"* James Madison **L3**

INSTRUCT

Develop Understanding
Anti-Federalists opposed ratification of the Constitution, insisting on the inclusion of a Bill of Rights to protect individual liberties. Review the reasons Federalists were able to win ratification despite this opposition.

Monitor Comprehension
Ask students why the anti-Federalists felt that a Bill of Rights needed to be included in the Constitution. Have them contrast the anti-Federalist argument with the Federalists'.

Targeted Resources

❏ Learning Styles Lesson Plan booklet, p. 13 **L2**
❏ Skills for Life booklet p. 7 **L1**
❏ Learning with Documents booklet, *The Federalist,* No. 71, p. 77 **L3**
❏ Presentation Pro CD-ROM, Chapter 5, Section 3 **L1**
❏ Exploring Primary Sources in U.S. History CD-ROM, *U.S. Constitution: The Bill of Rights; English Bill of Rights,* **L3**

ASSESS/RETEACH

Monitor Progress
Assess students completed graphic organizers using the Section Reading Support Transparency. Review the answers to the Guided Reading and Review worksheet.

Assess
Use the Section 3 Quiz to evaluate student understanding of key concepts in this section.

Reteach
Assign students the section summary in the Guide to the Essentials.

Targeted Resources

❏ Section Reading Support Transparency **L1** **ELL**
❏ Guided Reading and Review booklet, p. 22 **L1**
❏ Section 3 Quiz, Units 1/2 booklet, p. 55 **L1** **L2**
❏ Guide to the Essentials, p. 28 **L1** **L2**
❏ Social Studies Skills Tutor CD-ROM **L1**
❏ Guided Reading Audiotapes **ELL**
❏ Student Edition on Audio CD **ELL**

Homework _____

_____

Key
L1 Basic to Average   **L3** Average to Advanced
L2 For All Students   **ELL** English Language Learners

LESSON PLAN 5.4
The New Government
🕐 .5 Period, .25 Block

Section Objectives

1. Learn about the new leaders selected by President Washington.
2. Discover the challenges faced by Washington's government.
3. See the kinds of details that were involved in planning the capital city.

Vocabulary inauguration • Cabinet • domestic affairs • administration • precedent

Local Standards

FOCUS	**Targeted Resources**
Teach Key Concepts and Vocabulary The Constitution served as a blueprint for the new government. It was now up to the first president and Congress to make it work. **Build Background Knowledge** Ask students why officials were so concerned with the image of the president and the national capital.	❏ Activating Prior Knowledge, TE p. 165 **L1**

INSTRUCT	**Targeted Resources**
Develop Understanding President Washington and Congress were setting important precedents with every decision they made in running the new government. **Monitor Comprehension** Review with students George Washington's greatest challenges and achievements as the first president of the United States.	❏ Biography, Literature, and Comparing Primary Sources booklet, *Pierre-Charles L'Enfant*, p. 10 **L3** ❏ Presentation Pro CD-ROM, Chapter 5, Section 4 **L1**

ASSESS/RETEACH	**Targeted Resources**
Monitor Progress Assess students completed graphic organizers using the Section Reading Support Transparency. Review the answers to the Guided Reading and Review worksheet. **Assess** Use the Section 4 Quiz to evaluate student understanding of key concepts in this section. **Reteach** Assign students the section summary in the Guide to the Essentials.	❏ Section Reading Support Transparency **L1** **ELL** ❏ Guided Reading and Review booklet, p. 23 **L1** ❏ Section 4 Quiz, Units 1/2 booklet, p. 56 **L1** **L2** ❏ Guide to the Essentials, p. 29 **L1** **L2** ❏ Chapter Summary, Unit 1/2 booklet, p. 52 **L1** **ELL** ❏ GoOnline: PHSchool.com, Chapter 5 Self-Test, Web Code: mra-2055 ❏ Chapter 5 Tests, Units 1/2 booklet, pp. 57, 60

Homework _____

_____

Key

L1 Basic to Average	**L3** Average to Advanced
L2 For All Students	**ELL** English Language Learners

Teacher_____ Class _____ Date_____ M T W T F

LESSON PLAN 6.1
Liberty Versus Order in the 1790s
🕐 *1 Period, .5 Block*

Section Objectives   ## Local Standards

1. Learn about Alexander Hamilton's program for dealing with national and state debt.
2. Find out how foreign policy issues divided Americans.
3. See what issues led to the emergence of political parties.

Vocabulary tariff • interest • strict construction • loose construction • neutral • Jay's Treaty • Whiskey Rebellion • political party

FOCUS   **Targeted Resources**

Teach Key Concepts and Vocabulary
New political parties formed to oppose the policies of the Federalist-dominated government.

❏ Activating Prior Knowledge, TE p. 200 **L1**

❏ Sounds of an Era Audio CD, *Farewell Address, George Washington* **L3**

Build Background Knowledge
Despite its majority in Congress, the Federalist party had strong regional differences internally.

INSTRUCT   **Targeted Resources**

Develop Understanding
Review with students the major differences between the Federalist Party and the Jeffersonian Republicans.

❏ Learning Styles Lesson Plan booklet, p. 14 **L2**

❏ Presentation Pro CD-ROM, Chapter 6, Section 1 **L1**

Monitor Comprehension
Ask students to write a brief profile of a fictitious politician of the 1790s. Have them include his view on the Constitution, debt, business, army, political power, the British and French, and what his occupation is. This character should be identifiable as a Federalist or Jeffersonian Republican based on these traits.

❏ Exploring Primary Sources in U.S. History CD-ROM, *Farewell Address, George Washington* **L3**

❏ Prentice Hall U.S. History Video Collection, Vol. 5, *A New Nation (1776–1815)* **L2**

ASSESS/RETEACH   **Targeted Resources**

Monitor Progress
Assess students completed graphic organizers using the Section Reading Support Transparency. Review the answers to the Guided Reading and Review worksheet.

❏ Section Reading Support Transparency **L1** **ELL**

❏ Guided Reading and Review booklet, p. 24 **L1**

Assess
Use the Section 1 Quiz to evaluate student understanding of key concepts in this section.

❏ Section 1 Quiz, Units 1/2 booklet, p. 64 **L1** **L2**

❏ Guide to the Essentials, p. 31 **L1** **L2**

Reteach
Assign students the Guide to the Essentials.

❏ Guided Reading Audiotapes **ELL**

❏ Student Edition on Audio CD **ELL**

Homework _____
_____

Key
L1 Basic to Average   **L3** Average to Advanced
L2 For All Students   **ELL** English Language Learners

LESSON PLAN 6.2

The Election of 1800

1 Period, .5 Block

Section Objectives

1. Find out what actions John Adams took as President.
2. See why the election of 1800 was a turning point.
3. Discover what was significant about the transfer of power between parties in 1801.

Vocabulary XYZ affair • Alien and Sedition Acts • Virginia and Kentucky Resolutions

FOCUS	**Targeted Resources**

Teach Key Concepts and Vocabulary
Power was peacefully transferred from the Federalists to the Jeffersonian-Republicans in the election of 1800.

❑ Activating Prior Knowledge, TE p. 207 **L1**

Build Background Knowledge
The election of Jefferson over Adams demonstrated a "revolution in the principles of our government," according to Jefferson.

INSTRUCT	**Targeted Resources**

Develop Understanding
Jefferson's opposition to the Alien and Sedition Acts led him to victory in the election of 1800.

❑ Learning Styles Lesson Plan booklet, p. 15 **L2**

❑ Presentation Pro CD-ROM, Chapter 6, Section 2 **L1**

Monitor Comprehension
Have students list some of the ways in which Jefferson's presidency differed from his Federalist predecessors'.

ASSESS/RETEACH	**Targeted Resources**

Monitor Progress
Assess students completed graphic organizers using the Section Reading Support Transparency. Review the answers to the Guided Reading and Review worksheet.

❑ Section Reading Support Transparency **L1** **ELL**

❑ Guided Reading and Review booklet, p. 25 **L1**

❑ Section 2 Quiz, Units 1/2 booklet, p. 65 **L1** **L2**

Assess
Use the Section 2 Quiz to evaluate student understanding of key concepts in this section.

❑ Guide to the Essentials, p. 32 **L1** **L2**

❑ Social Studies Skills Tutor CD-ROM **L1**

Reteach
Assign students the section summary in the Guide to the Essentials.

❑ Guided Reading Audiotapes **ELL**

❑ Student Edition on Audio CD **ELL**

Homework _____

_____

Key
L1 Basic to Average **L3** Average to Advanced
L2 For All Students **ELL** English Language Learners

LESSON PLAN 6.3

The Jefferson Administration

🕐 *1 Period, .5 Block*

Section Objectives

1. Discover how Jefferson reduced the power of the national government.
2. See what problem Jefferson had with the federal courts.
3. Find out how Jefferson achieved his program in the West.
4. Learn why Jefferson easily won reelection in 1804.
5. Understand how Jefferson responded to increasing tensions with Europe.

Vocabulary agenda • bureaucracy • midnight judge • *Marbury* v. *Madison* • judicial review • Louisiana Purchase • Lewis and Clark expedition • embargo

Local Standards

FOCUS	**Targeted Resources**

Teach Key Concepts and Vocabulary
Ask students how Jefferson used his powers as President.

Build Background Knowledge
Remind students of Jefferson's goal of reducing the power of the federal government.

❑ Activating Prior Knowledge, TE p. 213 **L1**
❑ Color Transparencies, Historical Maps, A9, A60, A10 **L2**
❑ Historical Outline Map Book, *Political United States*, p. 82; *Exploring the Louisiana Purchase*, p. 30 **L1**

INSTRUCT	**Targeted Resources**

Develop Understanding
Jefferson used his power as President to limit the national government. Discuss the specific policies he adopted that made him popular with voters.

Monitor Comprehension
Ask students' to explain how the Louisiana Purchase was one way in which Jefferson both used and expanded, rather than limited, the power of national government.

❑ Skills for Life booklet, p. 8 **L1**
❑ Presentation Pro CD-ROM, Chapter 6, Section 3 **L1**

ASSESS/RETEACH	**Targeted Resources**

Monitor Progress
Assess students completed graphic organizers using the Section Reading Support Transparency.

Assess
Use the Section 3 Quiz to evaluate student understanding of key concepts in this section.

Reteach
Assign students the Guide to the Essentials.

❑ Section Reading Support Transparency **L1** **ELL**
❑ Guided Reading and Review booklet, p. 26 **L1**
❑ Section 3 Quiz, Units 1/2 booklet, p. 66 **L1** **L2**
❑ Guide to the Essentials, p. 33 **L1** **L2**
❑ Social Studies Skills Tutor CD-ROM **L1**
❑ Guided Reading Audiotapes **ELL**

Homework _____

_____

Key
L1 Basic to Average   **L3** Average to Advanced
L2 For All Students   **ELL** English Language Learners

LESSON PLAN 6.4

Native American Resistance

🕐 *.5 Period, .25 Block*

Section Objectives	**Local Standards**

Section Objectives

1. Find out what led to war between the United States and Native Americans in the Old Northwest.
2. See the different ways in which Native American leaders reacted to United States expansion.

Vocabulary Battle of Fallen Timbers • Treaty of Greenville • reservation • assimilation • Battle of Tippecanoe

FOCUS

Targeted Resources

Teach Key Concepts and Vocabulary
How successful were Native Americans in dealing with an expanding United States?

Build Background Knowledge
Cultural and linguistic differences between Native American groups would have made it difficult for them to form a united front against the United States.

❏ Activating Prior Knowledge, TE p. 220 **L1**

INSTRUCT

Targeted Resources

Develop Understanding
Different Native American leaders had different ways for dealing with United States expansion into their lands: accepting white culture, assimilating, returning to traditional culture, and taking military action.

Monitor Comprehension
Ask students to compare the ideas of the major Native American leaders of the Old Northwest during this period.

❏ Learning with Documents booklet, *Native American Politics*, p. 11 **L3**

❏ Biography, Literature, and Comparing Primary Sources booklet, *William Henry Harrison*, p. 11 **L3**

❏ Presentation Pro CD-ROM, Chapter 6, Section 4 **L1**

❏ Exploring Primary Sources in U.S. History CD-ROM, *Sell a Country! Why Not Sell the Air?* Tecumseh, **L3**

ASSESS/RETEACH

Targeted Resources

Monitor Progress
Assess students completed graphic organizers using the Section Reading Support Transparency. Review the answers to the Guided Reading and Review worksheet.

Assess
Use the Section 4 Quiz to evaluate student understanding of key concepts in this section.

Reteach
Assign students the Guide to the Essentials.

❏ Section Reading Support Transparency **L1** **ELL**

❏ Guided Reading and Review booklet, p. 27 **L1**

❏ Section 4 Quiz, Units 1/2 booklet, p. 67 **L1** **L2**

❏ Guide to the Essentials, p. 34 **L1** **L2**

❏ Social Studies Skills Tutor CD-ROM **L1**

❏ Student Edition on Audio CD **ELL**

Homework _____

_____

Key

L1 Basic to Average	**L3** Average to Advanced
L2 For All Students	**ELL** English Language Learners

LESSON PLAN 6.5

The War of 1812

🕐 *1 Period, .5 Block*

Section Objectives

1. Find out why war broke out with Britain in 1812.
2. See how the war's end affected the United States.
3. Understand events that led tot he economic panic of 1819.
4. Learn about issues that led to the Missouri Compromise.

Vocabulary impressment • War of 1812 • Treaty of Ghent • Battle of New Orleans • depression • Missouri Compromise

Local Standards

FOCUS

Teach Key Concepts and Vocabulary
What did Congress hope to gain by declaring war on Great Britain?

Build Background Knowledge
Ask students to recall what they already know about relations between the United States and Great Britain in the early 1800s.

Targeted Resources

- ❏ Activating Prior Knowledge, TE p. 224 **L1**
- ❏ Color Transparencies, Historical Maps, A11 **L2**
- ❏ Historical Outline Map Book, *The War of 1812*, p. 32; *The Missouri Compromise, 1820*, p. 45 **L1**
- ❏ Sounds of an Era Audio CD, *The Star-Spangled Banner* **L3**

INSTRUCT

Develop Understanding
Have students create a time line of major events in the War of 1812. Ask students how the Battle of New Orleans united the country and helped restore patriotism.

Monitor Comprehension
Did the United States meet its objectives at the end of the war? Explain. What unlooked for outcomes were achieved?

Targeted Resources

- ❏ Learning with Documents booklet, "*The Present State of Our Country*," p. 45; *The Star-Spangled Banner*, p. 78 **L3**
- ❏ Biography, Literature, and Comparing Primary Sources booklet, *An Illustrious Career*, p. 45–46; *For and Against the War of 1812*, pp. 107–108 **L3**
- ❏ Exploring Primary Sources in U.S. History CD-ROM, *On the Burning of Washington, D.C.*, *Dolley Madison*; *The Star-Spangled Banner*, *Francis Scott Key*, **L3**

ASSESS/RETEACH

Monitor Progress
Assess students completed graphic organizers using the Section Reading Support Transparency.

Assess
Use the Section 5 Quiz to evaluate student understanding of key concepts in this section.

Reteach
Assign students the Guide to the Essentials.

Targeted Resources

- ❏ Reading Support Transparency **L1 ELL**
- ❏ Guided Reading and Review booklet, p. 28 **L1**
- ❏ Section 5 Quiz, Units 1/2 booklet, p. 68 **L1 L2**
- ❏ Guide to the Essentials, p. 35 **L1 L2**
- ❏ GoOnline: PHSchool.com, Chapter 6 Self-Test, Web Code: mra-2066
- ❏ Chapter 6 Tests, Units 1/2 booklet, pp. 69, 72

Homework _____

_____

Key
L1 Basic to Average	**L3** Average to Advanced
L2 For All Students	**ELL** English Language Learners

LESSON PLAN 7.1

Cultural, Social, and Religious Life

🕐 *1 Period, .5 Block*

Section Objectives

1. Find out how Americans tried to advance the culture of the new nation.
2. Learn about some important social changes of the early 1800s.
3. See how a renewal of religious faith affected protestant churches.

Vocabulary republican virtues • mobile society • Second Great Awakening • evangelical • congregation • revival • denomination

Local Standards

FOCUS

Teach Key Concepts and Vocabulary
How did the rules of society change to meet the needs of the changing nation in the early 1800s?

Build Background Knowledge
Have students recall what they know about the first Great Awakening.

Targeted Resources

❏ Activating Prior Knowledge, TE p. 240 **L1**
❏ Sounds of an Era Audio CD, *"Sacred Harp,"* 1942; *"Free at Last"* **L3**

INSTRUCT

Develop Understanding
The movement of the population put new strains on social relations in the early 1800s. New social rules emerged to deal with these strains and set the stage for a Second Great Awakening.

Monitor Comprehension
Have students explore the new religious movement. How did it serve the new social order? Why did it appeal to women? How did it reflect democratic ideals?

Targeted Resources

❏ Learning Styles Lesson Plan booklet, p. 16 **L2**
❏ Learning with Documents booklet, *Do They Miss Me at Home?* p. 46; *The American Spirit,* p. 12 **L3**
❏ Presentation Pro CD-ROM, Chapter 7, Section 1 **L1**
❏ Prentice Hall U.S. History Video Collection, Vol. 6, *Expansionism* **L2**

ASSESS/RETEACH

Monitor Progress
Assess students' completed graphic organizers using the Section Reading Support Transparency. Review the answers to the Guided Reading and Review worksheet.

Assess
Use the Section 1 Quiz to evaluate student understanding of key concepts in this section.

Reteach
Assign students the Guide to the Essentials.

Targeted Resources

❏ Section Reading Support Transparency **L1 ELL**
❏ Guided Reading and Review booklet, p. 29 **L1**
❏ Section 1 Quiz, Units 3/4 booklet, p. 4 **L1 L2**
❏ Guide to the Essentials, p. 37 **L1 L2**
❏ Social Studies Skills Tutor CD-ROM **L1**
❏ Guided Reading Audiotapes **ELL**
❏ Student Edition on Audio CD **ELL**

Homework _____

_____

Key

L1	Basic to Average	**L3**	Average to Advanced
L2	For All Students	**ELL**	English Language Learners

LESSON PLAN 7.2

Trails to the West

🕐 *1 Period, .5 Block*

Section Objectives

1. Discover how and why settlers crossed the Appalachians.
2. See how the United States expanded into Florida.
3. Find out about factors that motivated American migrants bound for the Pacific.

Local Standards

Vocabulary trans- Appalachians • Adams-Onís Treaty • cede • manifest destiny • mountain man • Oregon Trail •pass • Santa Fe Trail • California Gold Rush • ghost town

---

FOCUS

Teach Key Concepts and Vocabulary
An adventurous generation of Americans crossed the continent looking for room to expand its ever-growing population.

Build Background Knowledge
Have students compile a list of reasons why Americans were motivated to migrate west of the Appalachians.

Targeted Resources

❑ Activating Prior Knowledge, TE p. 249 **L1**
❑ Color Transparencies, Historical Maps, A60 **L2**
❑ Historical Outline Map Book, *Western Land Claims*, p. 29; *The War of 1812*, p. 32; *Oregon Country*, p. 38; *Trails to the West*, p. 40; *Land Acquired from Native Americans to 1810*, p. 31 **L1**
❑ Sounds of an Era Audio CD *Morris Birkbeck on America Moving Westward* **L3**

INSTRUCT

Develop Understanding
Americans crossed the Appalachians and moved into the Ohio and Mississippi river valleys. Native Americans were forced to migrate by this expansion.

Monitor Comprehension
Have students compare reasons settlers first migrated to the Americas with reasons Americans began migrating west in the early 1800s.

Targeted Resources

❑ Learning Styles Lesson Plan booklet, p. 17 **L2**
❑ Skills for Life booklet, p. 9 **L1**
❑ Biography, Literature, and Comparing Primary Sources booklet, *On Peace and Friendship*, pp. 109–110; *The Pioneers*, pp. 47–48; *Brigham Young*, p. 12 **L3**
❑ Presentation Pro CD-ROM, Chapter 7, Section 2 **L1**

ASSESS/RETEACH

Monitor Progress
Assess students' completed graphic organizers using the Section Reading Support Transparency.

Assess
Use the Section 2 Quiz to evaluate student understanding of key concepts in this section.

Reteach
Assign students the Guide to the Essentials.

Targeted Resources

❑ Section Reading Support Transparency **L1** **ELL**
❑ Guided Reading and Review booklet, p. 30 **L1**
❑ Section 2 Quiz, Units 3/4 booklet, p. 5 **L1** **L2**
❑ Guide to the Essentials, p. 38 **L1** **L2**
❑ Social Studies Skills Tutor CD-ROM **L1**
❑ Guided Reading Audiotapes **ELL**

Homework _____

_____

Key
L1 Basic to Average   **L3** Average to Advanced
L2 For All Students   **ELL** English Language Learners

LESSON PLAN 7.3

The Great Plains and the Southwest

⏱ *1 Period, .5 Block*

Section Objectives

1. Learn how the lives of Plains Indians changed form the 1500s to the 1800s.
2. Discover how Spain integrated California and the Rio Grande valley into Hispanic North America.
3. Find out why Texas fought to win its independence from Mexico.

Vocabulary Great Plains • nomadic • presidio • Texas War for Independence • Battle of the Alamo

Local Standards

FOCUS

Teach Key Concepts and Vocabulary
Ask students how the migration of Spaniards from central Mexico and settlers from the United States into the Great Plains, California, and Texas caused tension between the United States and Mexico.

Build Background Knowledge
Discuss the effect of Spanish interaction with Native Americans of the Great Plains prior to American migration west.

Targeted Resources
❑ Activating Prior Knowledge, TE p. 258 **L1**
❑ Color Transparencies, Historical Maps, A16 **L2**
❑ Historical Outline Map Book, *Independence for Texas*, p. 39 **L1**

INSTRUCT

Develop Understanding
Ask students: What role did economics play in American colonization of Mexico's northern territories?

Monitor Comprehension
Have students list some political and economic changes resulting from Spanish and American migration into the Great Plains area.

Targeted Resources
❑ Presentation Pro CD-ROM, Chapter 7, Section 3 **L1**
❑ Exploring Primary Sources in U.S. History CD-ROM, *Letter from the Alamo*, Lt. Col. Comd't. William Barrett Travis **L3**

ASSESS/RETEACH

Monitor Progress
Assess students' completed graphic organizers using the Section Reading Support Transparency.

Assess
Use the Section 3 Quiz to evaluate student understanding of key concepts in this section.

Reteach
Assign students the Guide to the Essentials.

Targeted Resources
❑ Section Reading Support Transparency **L1 ELL**
❑ Guided Reading and Review booklet, p. 31 **L1**
❑ Section 3 Quiz, Units 3/4 booklet, p. 6 **L1 L2**
❑ Guide to the Essentials, p. 39 **L1 L2**
❑ Chapter Summary, Units 3/4 booklet, p. 3 **L1 ELL**
❑ GoOnline: PHSchool.com, Chapter 7 Self-Test, Web Code: mra-3074
❑ Chapter 7 Tests, Units 3/4 booklet, pp. 7, 10

Homework _____

_____

Key
L1 Basic to Average   **L3** Average to Advanced
L2 For All Students   **ELL** English Language Learners

LESSON PLAN 8.1

Inventions and Innovations

🕐 *1 Period, .5 Block*

Section Objectives

1. Find out how the Industrial Revolution arrived and spread in the United States, and learn about its impact.
2. Discover how improvements in transportation and communication changed American society.
3. Learn how the U.S. economy expanded during the early 1800s.
4. Read about the role banks had in the growth of the U.S. economy

Vocabulary Industrial Revolution • interchangeable parts • cotton gin • patent • Market Revolution • manufacturing • centralized • free enterprise system • specialization • investment capital • bank note

Local Standards

FOCUS

Teach Key Concepts and Vocabulary
Describe how the American Revolution also marked an era of social change that included a new spirit of innovation and experimentation.

Build Background Knowledge
Make a list of ways in which Americans tried to improve their lives in the early 1800s.

Targeted Resources

❑ Activating Prior Knowledge, TE p. 272 **L1**
❑ Historical Outline Map Book, *Transportation to the West*, p. 33 **L1**

INSTRUCT

Develop Understanding
Discuss with students the link between changes in technology and changes in social values. How did rapid change, progress, and improvement change people's thinking?

Monitor Comprehension
Discuss the effect the Industrial Revolution had on the U.S. economy.

Targeted Resources

❑ Biography, Literature, and Comparing Primary Sources booklet, *Catherine Littlefield Greene*, p. 13 **L3**

❑ Exploring Primary Sources in U.S. History CD-ROM, *A Description of Factory Life in 1846*, **L3**

❑ Prentice Hall U.S. History Video Collection, Vol. 7, *Democracy and Reform*; Vol. 8, *Causes of the Civil War*; Vol. 11, *Industrialization and Urbanization* **L2**

ASSESS/RETEACH

Monitor Progress
Assess students' completed graphic organizers using the Section Reading Support Transparency.

Assess
Use the Section 1 Quiz to evaluate student understanding of key concepts in this section.

Reteach
Assign students the Guide to the Essentials.

Homework _____

_____

Targeted Resources

❑ Section Reading Support Transparency **L1** **ELL**
❑ Guided Reading and Review booklet, p. 32 **L1**
❑ Section 1 Quiz, Units 3/4 booklet, p. 14 **L1** **L2**
❑ Guide to the Essentials, p. 41 **L1** **L2**

Key
L1 Basic to Average
L2 For All Students
L3 Average to Advanced
ELL English Language Learners

LESSON PLAN 8.2

The Northern Section

⏱ .5 Period, .25 Block

Section Objectives	**Local Standards**

Section Objectives

1. Understand how farming developed in the Old Northwest.
2. See which new industries arose in the Northeast.
3. Find out what caused the growth of cities, and what problems arose as they grew.
4. Learn what kinds of labor disputes arose in factories.

Vocabulary section • rural • urban • industrialization • tenement • strike • labor union

FOCUS

Targeted Resources

Teach Key Concepts and Vocabulary
Although most northerners were farmers, cities began growing rapidly during this period. What significant economic and social changes were taking place?

❏ Activating Prior Knowledge, TE p. 280 **L1**

Build Background Knowledge
Discuss with students the economic and social changes begun by the Market Revolution.

INSTRUCT

Targeted Resources

Develop Understanding
Discuss the changing nature of work for both farmers in the Old Northwest and for workers in the industrial Northeast. What new problems did these changes bring?

❏ Presentation Pro CD-ROM, Chapter 8, Section 2 **L1**

Monitor Comprehension
Have students debate the pros and cons of industrial development as they relate to the Northern Section in the early 1800s.

ASSESS/RETEACH

Targeted Resources

Monitor Progress
Assess students' completed graphic organizers using the Section Reading Support Transparency.

❏ Section Reading Support Transparency **L1** **ELL**

Assess
Use the Section 2 Quiz to evaluate student understanding of key concepts in this section.

❏ Guided Reading and Review booklet, p. 33 **L1**

❏ Section 2 Quiz, Unit 3/4 booklet, p. 15 **L1** **L2**

❏ Guide to the Essentials, p. 42 **L1** **L2**

Reteach
Assign students the Guide to the Essentials.

❏ Social Studies Skills Tutor CD-ROM **L1**

❏ Guided Reading Audiotapes **ELL**

❏ Student Edition on Audio CD **ELL**

Homework _____

_____

Key

L1 Basic to Average   **L3** Average to Advanced

L2 For All Students   **ELL** English Language Learners

31

Teacher_____ Class _____ Date_____ M T W T F

The Southern Section
🕐 .5 Period, .25 Block

Section Objectives

1. Learn how the economy of the South remained largely agricultural.
2. Find out how the lives of slaves differed on large and small farms.
3. Discover the results of slave revolts.

Vocabulary cotton belt • Turner's Rebellion

Local Standards

FOCUS

Teach Key Concepts and Vocabulary
The South's economy was centered on commercial agriculture. What was the South's most important crop?

Build Background Knowledge
Discuss with students how farming differed in the North and the South.

Targeted Resources
❑ Activating Prior Knowledge, TE p. 285 **L1**

INSTRUCT

Develop Understanding
As the South's dependence on commercial agriculture grew, so did its dependence on slave labor.

Monitor Comprehension
Ask students to explain how the growth of the southern economy affected the lives of enslaved Americans.

Targeted Resources
❑ Biography, Literature, and Comparing Primary Sources booklet, *The Confessions of Nat Turner*, p. 49 **L3**
❑ Presentation Pro CD-ROM, Chapter 8, Section 3 **L1**

ASSESS/RETEACH

Monitor Progress
Assess students' completed graphic organizers using the Section Reading Support Transparency. Review the answers to the Guided Reading and Review worksheet.

Assess
Use the Section 3 Quiz to evaluate student understanding of key concepts in this section.

Reteach
Assign students the section summary in the Guide to the Essentials.

Targeted Resources
❑ Section Reading Support Transparency **L1** **ELL**
❑ Guided Reading and Review booklet, p. 34 **L1**
❑ Section 3 Quiz, Unit 3/4 booklet, p. 16 **L1** **L2**
❑ Guide to the Essentials, p. 43 **L1** **L2**
❑ Social Studies Skills Tutor CD-ROM **L1**
❑ Guided Reading Audiotapes **ELL**
❑ Student Edition on Audio CD **ELL**

Homework _____

_____

Key
L1 Basic to Average   **L3** Average to Advanced
L2 For All Students   **ELL** English Language Learners

LESSON PLAN 8.4

The Growth of Nationalism

1 Period, .5 Block

Section Objectives

1. See some of the signs of a new nationalism after the War of 1812.
2. Find out why the election of 1824 was so controversial.
3. Discover what new political parties emerged in 1828, and find out what views they represent.

Vocabulary *Dartmouth College* v. *Woodward* • *McCulloch* v. *Maryland* • *Gibbons* v. *Ogden* • Monroe Doctrine • American System

Local Standards

FOCUS

Teach Key Concepts and Vocabulary

The federal government adopted nationalist policies, seeking more power over the economy and giving rise to new political parties.

Build Background Knowledge

Review with students earlier debates over where power should lie—with the states or with the federal government.

Targeted Resources

❏ Activating Prior Knowledge, TE p. 290 **L1**
❏ Historical Outline Map Book, *The United States in 1824*, p. 34; Election of 1828, p. 36 **L1**

INSTRUCT

Develop Understanding

Discuss how Jackson's defeat in the election of 1824 contributed to the formation of the National Republicans and Jacksonian Democrats. What were the major differences between these two parties?

Monitor Comprehension

Ask students to describe how the Supreme Court decisions of this period reflected the government's trend toward nationalism.

Targeted Resources

❏ Skills for Life booklet, p. 10 **L1**
❏ Learning with Documents booklet, *The Monroe Doctrine*, p. 79; *The Jackson Ticket*, p. 47 **L3**
❏ Presentation Pro CD-ROM, Chapter 8, Section 4 **L1**
❏ Exploring Primary Sources in U.S. History CD-ROM, *The Monroe Doctrine* **L2**

ASSESS/RETEACH

Monitor Progress

Assess students' completed graphic organizers using the Section Reading Support Transparency.

Assess

Use the Section 4 Quiz to evaluate student understanding of key concepts in this section.

Reteach

Assign students the section summary in the Guide to the Essentials.

Targeted Resources

❏ Section Reading Support Transparency **L1** **ELL**
❏ Guided Reading and Review booklet, p. 35 **L1**
❏ Section 4 Quiz, Unit 3/4 booklet, p. 17 **L1**
❏ Guide to the Essentials, p. 44 **L1** **L2**
❏ Social Studies Skills Tutor CD-ROM **L1**
❏ Guided Reading Audiotapes **ELL**

Homework _____

_____

Key
L1 Basic to Average   **L3** Average to Advanced
L2 For All Students   **ELL** English Language Learners

LESSON PLAN 8.5

The Age of Jackson

🕐 *1 Period, .5 Block*

Section Objectives

1. Understand how American government and democracy changed with Jackson as President.
2. Learn how Jackson responded to the tariff and Indian crises.
3. See what political strategies prompted the bank war.
4. Find out about the effectiveness of Jackson's presidential successors.

Local Standards

Vocabulary patronage • spoils system • Tariff of 1828 • nullify • states' rights • secede • Indian Removal Act • Trail of Tears • Black Hawk War • Second Seminole War

---

FOCUS

Teach Key Concepts and Vocabulary
How did Jackson use his terms in office to limit the power of the federal government?

Build Background Knowledge
Have students list Jackson's political positions prior to the 1828 election. How were these reflected in his actions as President?

Targeted Resources

❏ Activating Prior Knowledge, TE p. 297 **L1**
❏ Historical Outline Map Book, *Indian Removal, 1830–1842*, p. 37 **L1**
❏ Sounds of an Era Audio CD *Andrew Jackson on the Bank of the United States* **L3**

INSTRUCT

Develop Understanding
Have students make a list of the major events of Jackson's presidency. Ask students if Jackson's actions concerning these events were in accord with his philosophy of limited government.

Monitor Comprehension
How did Jackson limit the power of the federal government and strengthen the power of voters?

Targeted Resources

❏ Learning with Documents booklet, *President Jackson's Inauguration*, p. 13 **L3**
❏ Biography, Literature, and Comparing Primary Sources booklet, On *Webster* v. *Georgia*, pp. 111–112 **L3**
❏ Exploring Primary Sources in U.S. History CD-ROM, *Our Federal Union: It Must Be Preserved*, Andrew Jackson; *Debate Over Nullification, Daniel Webster and John C. Calhoun*, **L3**

ASSESS/RETEACH

Monitor Progress
Assess students' completed graphic organizers using the Section Reading Support Transparency.

Assess
Use the Section 5 Quiz to evaluate student understanding of key concepts in this section.

Reteach
Assign students the Guide to the Essentials.

Targeted Resources

❏ Section Reading Support Transparency **L1** **ELL**
❏ Guided Reading and Review booklet, p. 36 **L1**
❏ Section 5 Quiz, Units 3/4 booklet, p. 18 **L1** **L2**
❏ Guide to the Essentials, p. 45 **L1** **L2**
❏ GoOnline: PHSchool.com, Chapter 8 Self-Test, Web Code: mra-3086
❏ Chapter 8 Tests, Units 3/4 booklet, pp. 19, 22

Homework _____

_____

Key
L1 Basic to Average   **L3** Average to Advanced
L2 For All Students   **ELL** English Language Learners

LESSON PLAN 9.1
Reforming Society
⏱ *1 Period, .5 Block*

Section Objectives

1. Learn the message preached by Protestant revivalists.
2. Discover who the transcendentalists were.
3. Find out why reformers launched a temperance movement.
4. Understand how and why many reformers worked to improve society.

Local Standards

Vocabulary transcendentalism • temperance movement • abstinence • segregate • utopian community

FOCUS

Teach Key Concepts and Vocabulary
In what ways did reform-minded Americans address the country's social problems?

Build Background Knowledge
Protestant revivalists and transcendentalists shared the belief that individuals forged their own destinies.

Targeted Resources
❏ Activating Prior Knowledge, TE, p. 310 **L1**
❏ Sounds of an Era Audio CD, *"Self-Reliance,"* Ralph Waldo Emerson **L3**

INSTRUCT

Develop Understanding
Protestant reformers and transcendentalists sought to improve society through efforts such as the temperance movement, public education, and prison reform.

Monitor Comprehension
Have students compare and contrast the revivalists and the transcendentalists.

Targeted Resources
❏ Biography, Literature, and Comparing Primary Sources booklet, *On Property in Utopian Communities,* pp. 113–114 **L3**
❏ Exploring Primary Sources in U.S. History CD-ROM, *Civil Disobedience,* Henry David Thoreau; *Audubon and His Journals: My Style of Drawing Birds,* John James Audubon **L3**

ASSESS/RETEACH

Monitor Progress
Assess students completed graphic organizers using the Section Reading Support Transparency.

Assess
Use the Section 1 Quiz to evaluate student understanding of key concepts in this section.

Reteach
Assign students the Guide to the Essentials.

Targeted Resources
❏ Section Reading Support Transparency **L1** **ELL**
❏ Guided Reading and Review booklet, p. 37 **L1**
❏ Section 1 Quiz, Unit 3/4 booklet, p. 26 **L1** **L2**
❏ Guide to the Essentials, p. 47 **L1** **L2**
❏ Social Studies Skills Tutor CD-ROM **L1**
❏ Guided Reading Audiotapes **ELL**
❏ Student Edition on Audio CD **ELL**

Homework _____

_____

Key
L1 Basic to Average
L2 For All Students
L3 Average to Advanced
ELL English Language Learners

LESSON PLAN 9.2

The Antislavery Movement

⏱ *1 Period, .5 Block*

Section Objectives

1. Learn how the antislavery movement arose and grew.
2. Find out about contributions made by Frederick Douglass to the antislavery movement.
3. See what caused divisions to arise among abolitionists.
4. Discover how the Underground Railroad operated.
5. Understand how some Americans demonstrated resistance to abolitionism

Vocabulary abolitionist movement • emancipation • Underground Railroad • gag rule

Local Standards

FOCUS

Teach Key Concepts and Vocabulary
The debate over slavery included divisions within the antislavery movement itself. In what ways did abolitionists disagree?

Build Background Knowledge
As students read about abolitionists' tactics, have them rank them in order of riskiness.

Targeted Resources

❏ Activating Prior Knowledge, TE, p. 318 **L1**
❏ Color Transparencies, Historical Maps, A17 **L2**
❏ Sounds of an Era Audio CD, *The Narrative of the Life of an American Slave*, Frederick Douglass **L3**

INSTRUCT

Develop Understanding
Discuss the arguments for slavery, gradual abolition, and immediate abolition. Identify the supporters of each position.

Monitor Comprehension
Have students identify the tactics employed by abolitionists.

Targeted Resources

❏ Learning with Documents booklet, *Countrymen in Chains*, p. 48 **L3**
❏ Exploring Primary Sources in U.S. History CD-ROM, *Meaning of Fourth of July for the Negro*, Frederick Douglass **L3**
❏ American Heritage, My Brush with History, *The Underground Railroad*, Student Edition pp. 338–339, Videotape **L2**

ASSESS/RETEACH

Monitor Progress
Assess students completed graphic organizers using the Section Reading Support Transparency.

Assess
Use the Section 2 Quiz to evaluate student understanding of key concepts in this section.

Reteach
Assign students the Guide to the Essentials.

Targeted Resources

❏ Section Reading Support Transparency **L1** **ELL**
❏ Guided Reading and Review booklet, p. 38 **L1**
❏ Section 2 Quiz, Units 3/4 booklet, p. 27 **L1** **L2**
❏ Guide to the Essentials, p. 48 **L1** **L2**

Homework _____

_____

Key
L1 Basic to Average **L3** Average to Advanced
L2 For All Students **ELL** English Language Learners

LESSON PLAN 9.3

The Movement for Women's Rights

1 Period, .5 Block

Section Objectives

1. Find out what private roles women were expected to fulfill in the early 1800s.
2. Learn about the public roles gradually adopted by some women.
3. Discover the significance of the Seneca Falls Convention.

Vocabulary Seneca Falls Convention • suffrage

FOCUS

Teach Key Concepts and Vocabulary
In what ways did women reformers in the 1800s begin to challenge society's expectations for women?

Build Background Knowledge
Women in the early 1800s were relegated to the private sphere.

Targeted Resources

❏ Activating Prior Knowledge, TE, p. 326 **L1**
❏ Sounds of an Era Audio CD, *"Ain't I a Woman?"* Sojourner Truth **L3**

INSTRUCT

Develop Understanding
Catharine Beecher advocated reform within the private sphere, while reformers like Elizabeth Cady Stanton envisioned public roles for women.

Monitor Comprehension
Have students discuss some of the barriers women faced as they advocated for social change.

Targeted Resources

❏ Learning with Documents booklet, *Seneca Falls Declaration*, p. 80 **L3**
❏ Biography, Literature, and Comparing Primary Sources booklet, *Maria Mitchell*, p. 14 **L3**
❏ Presentation Pro CD-ROM, Chapter 9, Section 3 **L1**
❏ Exploring Primary Sources in U.S. History CD-ROM, *Seneca Falls Declaration of Sentiments* **L3**

ASSESS/RETEACH

Monitor Progress
Assess students completed graphic organizers using the Section Reading Support Transparency. Review the answers to the Guided Reading and Review worksheet.

Assess
Use the Section 3 Quiz to evaluate student understanding of key concepts in this section.

Reteach
Assign students the section summary in the Guide to the Essentials.

Targeted Resources

❏ Section Reading Support Transparency **L1** **ELL**
❏ Guided Reading and Review booklet, p. 39 **L1**
❏ Section 3 Quiz, Units 3/4 booklet, p. 28 **L1** **L2**
❏ Guide to the Essentials, p. 49 **L1** **L2**
❏ Social Studies Skills Tutor CD-ROM **L1**
❏ Guided Reading Audiotapes **ELL**
❏ Student Edition on Audio CD **ELL**

Homework _____

Key
L1 Basic to Average   **L3** Average to Advanced
L2 For All Students   **ELL** English Language Learners

LESSON PLAN 9.4
Growing Divisions
🕐 .5 Period, .25 Block

Section Objectives

1. Read about some causes of the huge rise in immigration to the United States in the 1830s and 1840s.
2. See why reform movements heightened tensions between the North and the South.

Vocabulary Irish Potato Famine • naturalize • discrimination

Local Standards

FOCUS

Teach Key Concepts and Vocabulary
Ask students why middle-class reformers caused resentment in some segments of society.

Build Background Knowledge
The growing demand for cheap labor attracted immigrants and rural Americans to the cities.

Targeted Resources
❏ Activating Prior Knowledge, TE p. 332 **L1**

INSTRUCT

Develop Understanding
As the working class grew larger and society more diverse, rifts began to form. Resentment toward middle-class reformers and immigrants grew, while life in the North diverged further from life in the South.

Monitor Comprehension
How did reformers stir up tensions between the North and the South?

Targeted Resources
❏ Learning Styles Lesson Plan booklet, p. 21 **L2**
❏ Learning with Documents booklet, *Plantation Life*, p. 14 **L3**
❏ Biography, Literature, and Comparing Primary Sources booklet, *A First-Hand Account of the Potato Famine*, p. 50 **L3**
❏ Presentation Pro CD-ROM, Chapter 9, Section 4 **L1**

ASSESS/RETEACH

Monitor Progress
Assess students completed graphic organizers using the Section Reading Support Transparency. Review the answers to the Guided Reading and Review worksheet.

Assess
Use the Section 4 Quiz to evaluate student understanding of key concepts in this section.

Reteach
Assign students the Guide to the section summary in the Essentials.

Targeted Resources
❏ Section Reading Support Transparency **L1** **ELL**
❏ Guided Reading and Review booklet, p. 40 **L1**
❏ Section 4 Quiz, Units 3/4 booklet, p. 29 **L1** **L2**
❏ Guide to the Essentials, p. 50 **L1** **L2**
❏ Social Studies Skills Tutor CD-ROM **L1**
❏ Guided Reading Audiotapes **ELL**
❏ Student Edition on Audio CD **ELL**
❏ Chapter Summary, Units 3/4 booklet, p. 25 **L1** **ELL**
❏ GoOnline: PHSchool.com, Chapter 9 Self-Test, Web Code: mra-3095
❏ Chapter 9 Tests, Units 3/4 booklet, pp. 30, 33

Homework _____

_____

Key
L1 Basic to Average   **L3** Average to Advanced
L2 For All Students   **ELL** English Language Learners

LESSON PLAN 10.1
Two Nations
🕐 *.5 Period, .25 Block*

Section Objectives

1. Find out why some historians think the Civil War was unavoidable.
2. Discover arguments used by abolitionists against slavery.
3. Learn how Southerners viewed slavery.
4. Understand some important differences between the North and the South.

Vocabulary Union • prejudice • obsolete

Local Standards

FOCUS

Teach Key Concepts and Vocabulary
Why did the North and South grow increasingly divided during the 1850s?

Build Background Knowledge
Have students list the differences between the North and the South that caused tensions between the two regions.

Targeted Resources
- ❏ Activating Prior Knowledge, TE, p. 346 **L1**
- ❏ Sounds of an Era Audio CD, *"Fourth of July Speech,"* Frederick Douglass **L3**

INSTRUCT

Develop Understanding
The differences in the economies of the North and the South became more pronounced by the 1850s. So, too, did the differences in their attitudes toward slavery.

Monitor Comprehension
Based on the extent of the differences between the North and the South, do students believe the Civil War could have been averted?

Targeted Resources
- ❏ Learning Styles Lesson Plan booklet, p. 22 **L2**
- ❏ Biography, Literature, and Comparing Primary Sources booklet, *An Abolitionist Bestseller,* pp. 51–52 **L3**
- ❏ Presentation Pro CD-ROM, Chapter 10, Section 1 **L1**
- ❏ Prentice Hall U.S. History Video Collection, Vol. 8, *Causes of the Civil War* **L2**

ASSESS/RETEACH

Monitor Progress
Assess students completed graphic organizers using the Section Reading Support Transparency. Review the answers to the Guided Reading and Review worksheet.

Assess
Use the Section 1 Quiz to evaluate student understanding of key concepts in this section.

Reteach
Assign students the section summary in the Guide to the Essentials.

Targeted Resources
- ❏ Section Reading Support Transparency **L1** **ELL**
- ❏ Guided Reading and Review booklet, p. 41 **L1**
- ❏ Section 1 Quiz, Units 3/4 booklet, p. 41 **L1** **L2**
- ❏ Guide to the Essentials, p. 52 **L1** **L2**
- ❏ Social Studies Skills Tutor CD-ROM **L1**
- ❏ Guided Reading Audiotapes **ELL**
- ❏ Student Edition on Audio CD **ELL**

Homework _____

_____

Key
L1	Basic to Average	**L3**	Average to Advanced
L2	For All Students	**ELL**	English Language Learners

LESSON PLAN 10.2

The Mexican War and Slavery Extension

⏱ *.5 Period, .25 Block*

Section Objectives

1. Learn about events that led to the annexation of Texas.
2. Understand why the United States went to war with Mexico.
3. See why the Wilmot Proviso led to conflict.

Local Standards

Vocabulary manifest destiny • annex • Mexican War • Treaty of Guadalupe Hidalgo • Gadsden Purchase • Wilmot Proviso

FOCUS

Teach Key Concepts and Vocabulary
Why did the annexation of Texas provoke war with Mexico? How else did the United States extend its boundaries in the 1840s?

Build Background Knowledge
Southerners supported the annexation of Texas as a slave state, while Northerners opposed it, fearing an unfavorable shift in the balance of power.

Targeted Resources

❏ Activating Prior Knowledge, TE, p. 351 **L1**
❏ Color Transparencies, Historical Maps, A18 **L2**
❏ Historical Outline Map Book, *War with Mexico, 1846–1848*, p. 41 **L1**
❏ Sounds of an Era Audio CD, *"Sovinir de Porto Rico"* **L3**

INSTRUCT

Develop Understanding
Going to war with Mexico and acquiring land through the Gadsden Purchase, the United States widened its borders. The debate over the expansion of slavery heated up, as the North and South vied for political power.

Monitor Comprehension
Have students list the causes and effects of the Mexican War.

Targeted Resources

❏ Learning with Documents booklet, *The Annexation of Texas*, p. 49 **L3**
❏ Presentation Pro CD-ROM, Chapter 10, Section 2 **L1**

ASSESS/RETEACH

Monitor Progress
Assess students completed graphic organizers using the Section Reading Support Transparency. Review the answers to the Guided Reading and Review worksheet.

Assess
Use the Section 2 Quiz to evaluate student understanding of key concepts in this section.

Reteach
Assign students the section summary in the Guide to the Essentials.

Targeted Resources

❏ Section Reading Support Transparency **L1** **ELL**
❏ Guided Reading and Review booklet, p. 42 **L1**
❏ Section 2 Quiz, Units 3/4 booklet, p. 42 **L1** **L2**
❏ Guide to the Essentials, p. 53 **L1** **L2**
❏ Social Studies Skills Tutor CD-ROM **L1**
❏ Guided Reading Audiotapes **ELL**
❏ Student Edition on Audio CD **ELL**

Homework _____

_____

Key
L1 Basic to Average
L2 For All Students
L3 Average to Advanced
ELL English Language Learners

LESSON PLAN 10.3
New Political Parties
🕐 *1 Period, .5 Block*

Section Objectives	Local Standards

Section Objectives

1. Discover some effects of the Missouri Compromise.
2. Learn what was accomplished by the Compromise of 1850.
3. See how political parties changed in the 1850s.
4. Find out why Stephen Douglas proposed the Kansas-Nebraska Act.

Vocabulary Compromise of 1850 • Fugitive Slave Act • nativism • Kansas-Nebraska Act • popular sovereignty

FOCUS

Teach Key Concepts and Vocabulary
What new political parties emerged in response to the growing debate over slavery?

Build Background Knowledge
Review the economic conditions that led to the continuation of slavery in the South and the rise of immigration in the North.

Targeted Resources
❏ Activating Prior Knowledge, TE, p. 355 **L1**
❏ Color Transparencies, Historical Maps, A19 **L2**
❏ Historical Outline Map Book, *The Missouri Compromise, 1820*, p. 45; *The Compromise of 1850*, p. 46; *Growth of the United States to 1853*, p. 42; *Kansas-Nebraska Act, 1854*, p. 47 **L1**
❏ Sounds of an Era Audio CD, *John C. Calhoun for the Compromise of 1850* **L3**

INSTRUCT

Develop Understanding
Discuss with students the failure of the political system to resolve the issue of slavery. Why did John C. Calhoun believe that the national government was a threat to Southern interests?

Monitor Comprehension
Have students list the new political parties that emerged during this era and provide a brief description of each.

Targeted Resources
❏ Skills for Life booklet, p. 12 **L1**
❏ Presentation Pro CD-ROM, Chapter 10, Section 3 **L1**
❏ Exploring Primary Sources in U.S. History CD-ROM, *A Frontier Lady, Sarah Royce* **L3**

ASSESS/RETEACH

Monitor Progress
Assess students completed graphic organizers using the Section Reading Support Transparency.

Assess
Use the Section 3 Quiz to evaluate student understanding of key concepts in this section.

Reteach
Assign students the section summary in the Guide to the Essentials.

Targeted Resources
❏ Section Reading Support Transparency **L1** **ELL**
❏ Guided Reading and Review booklet, p. 43 **L1**
❏ Section 3 Quiz, Units 3/4 booklet, p. 43 **L1** **L2**
❏ Guide to the Essentials, p. 54 **L1** **L2**
❏ Social Studies Skills Tutor CD-ROM **L1**
❏ Student Edition on Audio CD **ELL**

Homework _____

_____

Key
L1 Basic to Average   **L3** Average to Advanced
L2 For All Students   **ELL** English Language Learners

LESSON PLAN 10.4
The System Fails
1 Period, .5 Block

Section Objectives

1. Learn why violence erupted in Kansas in the mid-1850s.
2. See how slavery affected national politics in this period.
3. Find out about problems caused by the Lecompton constitution.
4. Understand important issues discussed in the Lincoln-Douglas debates.
5. See how John Brown's raid increased tensions between the North and the South.

Vocabulary free soiler • *Dred Scott* v. *Sandford* • Lincoln-Douglas Debates • arsenal

Local Standards

FOCUS

Teach Key Concepts and Vocabulary
Ask students why tension between the North and the South increased between 1856 and 1860.

Build Background Knowledge
Explain how John Brown's raids escalated violence throughout Kansas Territory.

Targeted Resources
❏ Activating Prior Knowledge, TE, p. 363 **L1**
❏ Color Transparencies, Time Lines, C4 **L2**

INSTRUCT

Develop Understanding
Kansas Territory became a bloody battleground for proslavery and antislavery forces. Meanwhile, a constitutional battle was being fought in the Supreme Court with the Dred Scott decision.

Monitor Comprehension
Have students outline the main arguments of the proslavery and antislavery positions.

Targeted Resources
❏ Learning with Documents booklet, *An Interview with John Brown*, p. 15 **L3**
❏ Presentation Pro CD-ROM, Chapter 10, Section 4 **L1**
❏ Exploring Primary Sources in U.S. History CD-ROM, *Dred Scott* v. *Sandford* **L3**

ASSESS/RETEACH

Monitor Progress
Assess students completed graphic organizers using the Section Reading Support Transparency. Review the answers to the Guided Reading and Review worksheet.

Assess
Use the Section 4 Quiz to evaluate student understanding of key concepts in this section.

Reteach
Assign students the section summary in the Guide to the Essentials.

Targeted Resources
❏ Section Reading Support Transparency **L1** **ELL**
❏ Guided Reading and Review booklet, p. 44 **L1**
❏ Section 4 Quiz, Units 3/4 booklet, p. 44 **L1** **L2**
❏ Guide to the Essentials, p. 55 **L1** **L2**
❏ Social Studies Skills Tutor CD-ROM **L1**
❏ Guided Reading Audiotapes **ELL**
❏ Student Edition on Audio CD **ELL**

Homework _____

_____

Key
L1 Basic to Average
L2 For All Students
L3 Average to Advanced
ELL English Language Learners

LESSON PLAN 10.5

A Nation Divided Against Itself

⏱ *.5 Period, .25 Block*

Section Objectives

1. Find out how the election of 1860 demonstrated the split between the North and the South.
2. See what concerns led the Lower South to secede from the Union.
3. Discover the event that started the Civil War.

Local Standards

Vocabulary Border States • Lower South • secessionist • Confederate States of America • Fort Sumter • Upper South

---

FOCUS

Teach Key Concepts and Vocabulary
What provoked southern states to leave the Union in 1860?

Build Background Knowledge
As students read, have them create a timeline of events from the election of Lincoln to the firing on Fort Sumter.

Targeted Resources

❏ Activating Prior Knowledge, TE, p. 369 **L1**
❏ Historical Outline Map Book, *The Northern States*, p. 43; *Election of 1860*, p. 48; *The Southern States*, p. 44; *Choosing Sides*, p. 49 **L1**

INSTRUCT

Develop Understanding
Discuss Southerners' arguments for secession. Why was Lincoln's election an outrage to the South? Why did they feel withdrawal from the Union was legitimate?

Monitor Comprehension
What was Lincoln's dilemma regarding the defense of Fort Sumter?

Targeted Resources

❏ Learning Styles Lesson Plan booklet, p. 23 **L2**
❏ Biography, Literature, and Comparing Primary Sources booklet, *General P. G. T. Beauregard*, p. 15; *On Southern Secession*, pp. 115–116 **L3**
❏ Presentation Pro CD-ROM, Chapter 10, Section 5 **L1**

ASSESS/RETEACH

Monitor Progress
Assess students completed graphic organizers using the Section Reading Support Transparency. Review the answers to the Guided Reading and Review worksheet.

Assess
Use the Section 5 Quiz to evaluate student understanding of key concepts in this section.

Reteach
Assign students the section summary in the Guide to the Essentials.

Targeted Resources

❏ Section Reading Support Transparency **L1 ELL**
❏ Guided Reading and Review booklet, p. 45 **L1**
❏ Section 5 Quiz, Units 3/4 booklet, p. 45 **L1 L2**
❏ Guide to the Essentials, p. 56 **L1 L2**
❏ Chapter Summary, Units 4/5 booklet, p. 40 **L1 ELL**
❏ GoOnline: PHSchool.com, Chapter 10 Self-Test, Web Code: mra-4106
❏ Chapter 10 Tests, Units 3/4 booklet, pp. 46, 49

Homework _____

_____

Key
L1 Basic to Average   **L3** Average to Advanced
L2 For All Students   **ELL** English Language Learners

LESSON PLAN 11.1

From Bull Run to Antietam

🕐 *1 Period, .5 Block*

Section Objectives

1. Understand the significance of the First Battle of Bull Run.
2. Find out how the North and the South prepared for war.
3. Learn why the battles in the West were important.
4. Discover the outcome of each of the battles in the East in 1862.

Local Standards

Vocabulary Civil War • First Battle of Bull Run • casualty • war of attrition • shell • canister • Battle of Shiloh • Battle of Antietam

FOCUS

Teach Key Concepts and Vocabulary
How were the expectations of both sides called into question in the early days of the war?

Build Background Knowledge
Northerners believed capturing the Confederate capital would bring a quick end to the war.

Targeted Resources

❑ Activating Prior Knowledge, TE, p. 380 **L1**
❑ Historical Outline Map Book, *Choosing Sides*, p. 49; *The Civil War in the East*, p. 51; *Major Battles of the Civil War*, p. 50 **L1**
❑ Sounds of an Era Audio CD, *"The Iron Merrimack"* **L3**

INSTRUCT

Develop Understanding
Discuss with students how the first Battle of Bull Run changed people's way of thinking about the war. How did the lag between battle tactics and weapons technology affect the war?

Monitor Comprehension
Have students create a timeline of major battles of the first two years of the Civil War, noting the outcome of each battle.

Targeted Resources

❑ Biography, Literature, and Comparing Primary Sources booklet, *The First Battle of Bull Run*, p. 55; *On the Purpose of the Civil War*, p. 117 **L3**
❑ Presentation Pro CD-ROM, Chapter 11, Section 1 **L1**
❑ Exploring Primary Sources in U.S. History CD-ROM, *Civil War Photograph*, Mathew Brady **L3**
❑ Prentice Hall U.S. History Video Collection, Vol. 9, *The Civil War* **L2**

ASSESS/RETEACH

Monitor Progress
Assess students completed graphic organizers using the Section Reading Support Transparency.

Assess
Use the Section 1 Quiz to evaluate student understanding of key concepts in this section.

Reteach
Assign students the Guide to the Essentials.

Targeted Resources

❑ Section Reading Support Transparency **L1** **ELL**
❑ Guided Reading and Review booklet, p. 46 **L1**
❑ Section 1 Quiz, Units 3/4 booklet, p. 53 **L1** **L2**
❑ Guide to the Essentials, p. 58 **L1** **L2**
❑ Social Studies Skills Tutor CD-ROM **L1**

Homework _____

_____

Key
L1 Basic to Average   **L3** Average to Advanced
L2 For All Students   **ELL** English Language Learners

LESSON PLAN 11.2
Life Behind the Lines
🕐 *1 Period, .5 Block*

Section Objectives

1. Learn how wartime politics affected the Confederate and Union governments.
2. Discover how the Emancipation Proclamation affected both the North and the South.
3. Find out the causes and effects of African Americans' joining the Union Army.
4. List the kinds of hardships that befell the North and the South during the war.

Local Standards

Vocabulary draft • recognition • greenback • Copperhead • martial law • writ of *habeas corpus* • Emancipation Proclamation • contraband

---

FOCUS

Teach Key Concepts and Vocabulary
What kinds of changes did the Civil War bring to Northerners and Southerners?

Build Background Knowledge
Ask students to recall how the power of the federal government in the United States changed during its first century.

Targeted Resources
❏ Activating Prior Knowledge, TE, p. 390 **L1**
❏ Historical Outline Map Book, *The Southern States*, p. 44; *The Northern States*, p. 43 **L1**

INSTRUCT

Develop Understanding
Discuss the strengths and weaknesses of the Confederate government. Discuss how the Union government grew in power during the war. What extraordinary powers did Lincoln use to keep the Border States in the Union?

Monitor Comprehension
Identify Union emergency wartime actions and explain how they differed from other government actions, such as the Emancipation Proclamation or the establishment of a national currency.

Targeted Resources
❏ Skills for Life booklet, p. 13 **L1**
❏ Learning with Documents booklet, *The Emancipation Proclamation*, p. 81 **L3**
❏ Presentation Pro CD-ROM, Chapter 11, Section 2 **L1**
❏ Exploring Primary Sources in U.S. History CD-ROM, *The Education of Henry Adams: Foes or Friends*, Henry Adams **L3**
❏ American Heritage, My Brush with History, *A Civil War Soldier's Story*, Student Edition, pp. 420–421, Videotape **L2**

ASSESS/RETEACH

Monitor Progress
Assess students completed graphic organizers using the Section Reading Support Transparency.

Assess
Use the Section 2 Quiz to evaluate student understanding of key concepts in this section.

Reteach
Assign students the Guide to the Essentials.

Homework _____

_____

Targeted Resources
❏ Section Reading Support Transparency **L1** **ELL**
❏ Guided Reading and Review booklet, p. 47 **L1**
❏ Section 2 Quiz, Units 3/4 booklet, p. 54 **L1** **L2**
❏ Guide to the Essentials, p. 59 **L1** **L2**

Key
L1 Basic to Average **L3** Average to Advanced
L2 For All Students **ELL** English Language Learners

LESSON PLAN 11.3
The Tide of War Turns
🕐 *1 Period, .5 Block*

Section Objectives

1. Identify the importance of Lee's victories at Fredericksburg and Chancellorsville.
2. Describe how the Battles of Gettysburg and Vicksburg turned the tide of the war.
3. Find out why 1863 was a pivotal year in the Civil War.
4. Interpret the message of the Gettysburg Address.

Vocabulary Battle of Fredericksburg • Battle of Chancellorsville • Battle of Gettysburg • Pickett's Charge • siege • Gettysburg Address

Local Standards

FOCUS

Teach Key Concepts and Vocabulary
Why did the battles of Gettysburg and Vicksburg turn the tide of the war?

Build Background Knowledge
As students read, have them note General Lee's victories. What were Lee's strengths?

Targeted Resources
- ❏ Activating Prior Knowledge, TE, p. 402 **L1**
- ❏ Color Transparencies, Historical Maps, A2, A23 **L2**
- ❏ Historical Outline Map Book, *Major Battles of the Civil War*, p. 50 **L1**
- ❏ Sounds of an Era Audio CD, *The Gettysburg Address* **L3**

INSTRUCT

Develop Understanding
The capture of Vicksburg in 1863 divided the Confederacy in two. What was the significance of the Battle of Gettysburg?

Monitor Comprehension
Have students summarize the following battles and give the significance of each: Fredericksburg, Chancellorsville, Gettysburg, and Vicksburg.

Targeted Resources
- ❏ Learning Styles Lesson Plan booklet, p. 24 **L2**
- ❏ Learning with Documents booklet, *The Gettysburg Address*, p. 16 **L3**
- ❏ Presentation Pro CD-ROM, Chapter 11, Section 3 **L1**
- ❏ Exploring Primary Sources in U.S. History CD-ROM, *Gettysburg Address*, Abraham Lincoln **L3**

ASSESS/RETEACH

Monitor Progress
Assess students completed graphic organizers using the Section Reading Support Transparency. Review the answers to the Guided Reading and Review worksheet.

Assess
Use the Section 3 Quiz to evaluate student understanding of key concepts in this section.

Reteach
Assign students the section summary in the Guide to the Essentials.

Homework _____

_____

Targeted Resources
- ❏ Section Reading Support Transparency **L1** **ELL**
- ❏ Guided Reading and Review booklet, p. 48 **L1**
- ❏ Section 3 Quiz, Unit 3/4 booklet, p. 55 **L1** **L2**
- ❏ Guide to the Essentials, p. 60 **L1** **L2**
- ❏ Social Studies Skills Tutor CD-ROM **L1**
- ❏ Guided Reading Audiotapes **ELL**
- ❏ Student Edition on Audio CD **ELL**

Key
L1 Basic to Average   **L3** Average to Advanced
L2 For All Students   **ELL** English Language Learners

LESSON PLAN 11.4

Devastation and New Freedom

🕐 *1 Period, .5 Block*

Section Objectives

1. Determine General Grant's strategy for defeating the South and how he and General Sherman implemented it.
2. Outline the issues and results of the election of 1864.
3. Explain how the South was finally defeated on the battlefield.
4. State how and why John Wilkes Booth assassinated President Lincoln.

Vocabulary Battle of the Wilderness • Battle of Spotsylvania • Battle of Cold Harbor • Thirteenth Amendment

Local Standards

FOCUS

Teach Key Concepts and Vocabulary
What were the costs of the Civil War? What was achieved?

Build Background Knowledge
As students read Lincoln's Second Inaugural Address, have them consider how his words were an attempt to help the newly rejoined nation begin the process of reconciliation.

Targeted Resources
❑ Activating Prior Knowledge, TE, p. 410 **L1**
❑ Color Transparencies, Historical Maps, A20, A21, A24 **L2**
❑ Historical Outline Map Book, *Union Advances*, p. 52 **L1**

INSTRUCT

Develop Understanding
Discuss Grant's and Sherman's commitment to total war and its effect on the South. Ask students to describe the surrender at Appomattox Courthouse.

Monitor Comprehension
Ask students how Lincoln's reelection led to the passage of the Thirteenth Amendment.

Targeted Resources
❑ Learning Styles Lesson Plan booklet, p. 25 **L2**
❑ Learning with Documents booklet, *Defending Atlanta*, p. 50 **L3**
❑ Exploring Primary Sources in U.S. History CD-ROM, *Second Inaugural Address*, Abraham Lincoln **L3**

ASSESS/RETEACH

Monitor Progress
Assess students completed graphic organizers using the Section Reading Support Transparency. Review the answers to the Guided Reading and Review worksheet.

Assess
Use the Section 4 Quiz to evaluate student understanding of key concepts in this section.

Reteach
Assign students the Guide to the Essentials.

Targeted Resources
❑ Section Reading Support Transparency **L1 ELL**
❑ Guided Reading and Review booklet, p. 49 **L1**
❑ Section 4 Quiz, Units 3/4 booklet, p. 56 **L1 L2**
❑ Guide to the Essentials, p. 61 **L1 L2**
❑ Chapter Summary, Unit 3/4 booklet, p. 52 **L1 ELL**
❑ GoOnline: PHSchool.com, Chapter 11 Self-Test, Web Code: mra-4115
❑ Chapter 11 Tests, Units 3/4 booklet, pp. 57, 60 **ELL**

Homework _____

_____

Key
L1 Basic to Average   **L3** Average to Advanced
L2 For All Students   **ELL** English Language Learners

LESSON PLAN 12.1

Presidential Reconstruction

🕐 *1 Period, .5 Block*

Section Objectives

1. Learn about conditions in the South following the Civil War.
2. Analyze Lincoln's and Johnson's Reconstruction plans for similarities.
3. Find out how newly freed slaves began to rebuild their lives.

Vocabulary Reconstruction • pardon • Radical Republicans • pocket veto • Freedmen's Bureau

Local Standards

FOCUS

Teach Key Concepts and Vocabulary
What were the main issues of Reconstruction?

Build Background Knowledge
Discuss with students why a harsh Reconstruction plan might have increased Southern resentment toward the federal government.

Targeted Resources

❏ Activating Prior Knowledge, TE, p. 424 **L1**
❏ Historical Outline Map Book, *Reconstruction*, p. 53 **L1**
❏ Sounds of an Era Audio CD, *"When Johnny Comes Marching Home Again"* **L3**

INSTRUCT

Develop Understanding
Following the Civil War, the government had to find a way to put the nation back together, to deal with the enormous destruction suffered by the South, and to help newly freed slaves rebuild their lives. How did Lincoln's and Johnson's Reconstruction plans address these and other issues following the war?

Monitor Comprehension
Have students list, in order of importance, problems the nation faced during Reconstruction.

Targeted Resources

❏ Learning Styles Lesson Plan booklet, p. 26 **L2**
❏ Learning with Documents booklet, *A Symbol of Freedom*, p. 51 **L3**
❏ Biography, Literature, and Comparing Primary Sources booklet, *The Story of Free Joe*, pp. 54–56; *Charlotte Forten Grimké*, p. 17 **L3**
❏ Presentation Pro CD-ROM, Chapter 12, Section 1 **L1**
❏ Prentice Hall U.S. History Video Collection, Vol. 10, *Reconstruction and Segregation* **L2**

ASSESS/RETEACH

Monitor Progress
Assess students completed graphic organizers using the Section Reading Support Transparency. Review the answers to the Guided Reading and Review worksheet.

Assess
Use the Section 1 Quiz to evaluate student understanding of key concepts in this section.

Reteach
Assign students the section summary in the Guide to the Essentials.

Targeted Resources

❏ Section Reading Support Transparency **L1** **ELL**
❏ Guided Reading and Review booklet, p. 50 **L1**
❏ Section 1 Quiz, Unit 3/4 booklet, p. 64 **L1** **L2**
❏ Guide to the Essentials, p. 63 **L1** **L2**
❏ Social Studies Skills Tutor CD-ROM **L1**
❏ Guided Reading Audiotapes **ELL**
❏ Student Edition on Audio CD **ELL**

Homework _____
_____

Key
L1 Basic to Average   **L3** Average to Advanced
L2 For All Students   **ELL** English Language Learners

LESSON PLAN 12.2

Congressional Reconstruction

🕐 *1 Period, .5 Block*

Section Objectives

1. Discover how black codes and the Fourteenth Amendment were related.
2. Analyze the differences between Congress's Reconstruction plan and Andrew Johnson's.
3. Learn the significance of the Fifteenth Amendment.
4. Find out who supported the Republican governments of the South.

Local Standards

Vocabulary black codes • Fourteenth Amendment • civil rights • impeach • Fifteenth Amendment • carpetbagger • scalawag

FOCUS

Teach Key Concepts and Vocabulary
Why did Congress take over Reconstruction?

Build Background Knowledge
Explain that southern states began to enact black codes to undermine Reconstruction after they were readmitted to the Union under Johnson's plan.

Targeted Resources
❏ Activating Prior Knowledge, TE, p. 430 **L1**
❏ Sounds of an Era Audio CD, *Campaign Song for Ulysses S. Grant* **L3**

INSTRUCT

Develop Understanding
Discuss how congressional Republicans brought about radical political and social changes to the South. Why was Congress dissatisfied with Reconstruction under Johnson, and how did this dissatisfaction lead to his impeachment?

Monitor Comprehension
What was Congress hoping to accomplish by passing the Fourteenth and Fifteenth Amendments?

Targeted Resources
❏ Learning with Documents booklet, *Speeches by Blanche K. Bruce and Frederick Douglass*, p. 82 **L3**
❏ Biography, Literature, and Comparing Primary Sources booklet, *On Voting Rights for African Americans*, pp. 119–120 **L3**
❏ Presentation Pro CD-ROM, Chapter 12, Section 2 **L1**

ASSESS/RETEACH

Monitor Progress
Assess students completed graphic organizers using the Section Reading Support Transparency. Review the answers to the Guided Reading and Review worksheet.

Assess
Use the Section 2 Quiz to evaluate student understanding of key concepts in this section.

Reteach
Assign students the Guide to the Essentials.

Targeted Resources
❏ Section Reading Support Transparency **L1** **ELL**
❏ Guided Reading and Review booklet, p. 51 **L1**
❏ Section 2 Quiz, Unit 3/4 booklet, p. 65 **L1** **L2**
❏ Guide to the Essentials, p. 64 **L1** **L2**
❏ Social Studies Skills Tutor CD-ROM **L1**
❏ Guided Reading Audiotapes **ELL**
❏ Student Edition on Audio CD **ELL**

Homework _____

Key
L1 Basic to Average   **L3** Average to Advanced
L2 For All Students   **ELL** English Language Learners

LESSON PLAN 12.3

Birth of the "New South"

🕐 .5 Period, .25 Block

Section Objectives

1. Find out how farming in the South changed after the Civil War.
2. Explore how the growth of cities and industry began to change the South's economy after the war.
3. Learn how money designated for Reconstruction projects was used.

Local Standards

Vocabulary sharecropping • tenant farming • infrastructure

FOCUS	**Targeted Resources**

Teach Key Concepts and Vocabulary
What economic changes took place in the South after the Civil War?

Build Background Knowledge
As students read, have them track the good and bad effects of the government's method of economic redevelopment of the South.

❏ Activating Prior Knowledge, TE p. 436 **L1**

INSTRUCT	**Targeted Resources**

Develop Understanding
The end of slavery brought about new patterns of farming. State governments poured money into rebuilding infrastructure, and the region experienced limited industrial growth.

Monitor Comprehension
Have students list the economic challenges faced by the South after the Civil War. Which do they think was the greatest?

❏ Learning Styles Lesson Plan booklet, p. 27 **L2**
❏ Skills for Life booklet, p. 14 **L1**
❏ Learning with Documents booklet, *A Bleak Future for Freedmen*, p. 17 **L3**
❏ Presentation Pro CD-ROM, Chapter 12, Section 3 **L1**

ASSESS/RETEACH	**Targeted Resources**

Monitor Progress
Assess students completed graphic organizers using the Section Reading Support Transparency. Review the answers to the Guided Reading and Review worksheet.

Assess
Use the Section 3 Quiz to evaluate student understanding of key concepts in this section.

Reteach
Assign students the section summary in the Guide to the Essentials.

❏ Section Reading Support Transparency **L1** **ELL**
❏ Guided Reading and Review booklet, p. 52 **L1**
❏ Section 3 Quiz, Unit 3/4 booklet, p. 66 **L1** **L2**
❏ Guide to the Essentials, p. 65 **L1** **L2**
❏ Social Studies Skills Tutor CD-ROM **L1**
❏ Guided Reading Audiotapes **ELL**
❏ Student Edition on Audio CD **ELL**

Homework _____

_____

Key
L1 Basic to Average   **L3** Average to Advanced
L2 For All Students   **ELL** English Language Learners

LESSON PLAN 12.4

The End of Reconstruction

⏱ *.5 Period, .25 Block*

Section Objectives

1. Learn about tactics used by the Ku Klux Klan to spread terror throughout the South.
2. Find out why Reconstruction ended.
3. Review the major successes and failures of Reconstruction.

Local Standards

Vocabulary Enforcement Act of 1870 • solid South • Compromise of 1877

FOCUS

Teach Key Concepts and Vocabulary
Why did public support for Reconstruction wane?

Build Background Knowledge
Discuss how the southern backlash against Reconstruction turned violent. Explain how organizations like the Ku Klux Klan were able to prevent African Americans from exercising their legal rights.

Targeted Resources
❏ Activating Prior Knowledge, TE, p. 442 **L1**
❏ Historical Outline Map Book, *Election of 1876*, p. 54 **L1**

INSTRUCT

Develop Understanding
Analyze the loss of public support for Reconstruction. What finally brought Reconstruction to an end? Ask students if they think Reconstruction was a success or a failure.

Monitor Comprehension
In what ways did Reconstruction fail to achieve social equality for African Americans?

Targeted Resources
❏ Presentation Pro CD-ROM, Chapter 12, Section 4 **L1**

ASSESS/RETEACH

Monitor Progress
Assess studentscompleted graphic organizers using the Section Reading Support Transparency. Review the answers to the Guided Reading and Review worksheet.

Assess
Use the Section 4 Quiz to evaluate student understanding of key concepts in this section.

Reteach
Assign students the section summary in the Guide to the Essentials.

Targeted Resources
❏ Section Reading Support Transparency **L1** **ELL**
❏ Guided Reading and Review booklet, p. 53 **L1**
❏ Section 4 Quiz, Units 3/4 booklet, p. 67 **L1** **L2**
❏ Guide to the Essentials, p. 66 **L1** **L2**
❏ Chapter Summary, Unit 3/4 booklet, p. 63 **L1** **ELL**
❏ GoOnline: PHSchool.com, Chapter 12 Self-Test, Web Code: mra-4125
❏ Chapter 12 Tests, Unit 3/4 booklet, pp. 68, 71

Homework _____
_____

Key
L1 Basic to Average   **L3** Average to Advanced
L2 For All Students   **ELL** English Language Learners

LESSON PLAN 13.1

A Technological Revolution

⏱ *1 Period, .5 Block*

Section Objectives

1. Learn how daily lives changed in the decades following the Civil War.
2. Find out how advances in electric power and communication affected people and businesses in this era.
3. Discover the effects the development of railroads had on industrial growth.
4. Think about the impact of the Bessemer process on American culture.

Vocabulary patent • productivity • transcontinental railroad • Bessemer process • mass production

Local Standards

FOCUS

Teach Key Concepts and Vocabulary
How did inventions transform American life in the late nineteenth century?

Build Background Knowledge
Explain that conditions were ripe for a surge in technological progress: business leaders had capital to invest, natural resources were abundant, and great thinkers were churning out ideas.

Targeted Resources

❏ Activating Prior Knowledge, TE, p. 456 **L1**
❏ Historical Outline Map Book, *Political United States*, p. 82 **L1**
❏ Sounds of an Era Audio CD, *Thomas Edison on the Electric Age*, 1908 **L3**

INSTRUCT

Develop Understanding
Discuss with students the impact of technological innovations on the nature of work, the American labor movement, and business.

Monitor Comprehension
Ask students to give some examples of how new technologies revolutionized American life in the years after the Civil War.

Targeted Resources

❏ Learning Styles Lesson Plan booklet, p. 28 **L2**
❏ Skills for Life booklet, p. 15 **L1**
❏ Exploring Primary Sources in U.S. History CD-ROM, *The Tall Office Building Artistically Considered*, Louis H. Sullivan **L3**
❏ Prentice Hall U.S. History Video Collection, Vol. 11, *Industrialization and Urbanization* **L3**

ASSESS/RETEACH

Monitor Progress
Assess students completed graphic organizers using the Section Reading Support Transparency.

Assess
Use the Section 1 Quiz to evaluate student understanding of key concepts in this section.

Reteach
Assign students the section summary in the Guide to the Essentials.

Targeted Resources

❏ Section Reading Support Transparency **L1** **ELL**
❏ Guided Reading and Review booklet, p. 54 **L1**
❏ Section 1 Quiz, Units 5/6 booklet, p. 6 **L1 L2**
❏ Guide to the Essentials, p. 68 **L1 L2**
❏ Social Studies Skills Tutor CD-ROM **L1**
❏ Guided Reading Audiotapes **ELL**

Homework _____
_____

Key
L1 Basic to Average   **L3** Average to Advanced
L2 For All Students   **ELL** English Language Learners

LESSON PLAN 13.2
The Growth of Big Business
⏱ *1 Period, .5 Block*

Section Objectives

1. Read to find out why American industrialists of the late 1800s were called both "robber barons" and "captains of industry."
2. Discover how social Darwinism affected Americans' views on big business.
3. Analyze the ways in which big businesses differed from smaller businesses.
4. Learn how industrialists gained a competitive edge over their rivals.

Vocabulary social Darwinism • oligopoly • monopoly • cartel • vertical consolidation • economies of scale • horizontal consolidation • trust • Sherman Antitrust Act

Local Standards

FOCUS

Teach Key Concepts and Vocabulary
What organizational changes did big businesses undergo in the late nineteenth century?

Build Background Knowledge
Ask students why industrialists advocated the theory of social Darwinism.

Targeted Resources
❑ Activating Prior Knowledge, TE, p. 467 **L1**
❑ Sounds of an Era Audio CD, *"Gospel of Wealth"* **L3**

INSTRUCT

Develop Understanding
Powerful industrialists of the late 1800s transformed their businesses into giant enterprises. Discuss how these men can be viewed as both captains of industry and robber barons.

Monitor Comprehension
Ask students to discuss the pros and cons of the growth of big business in the late 1800s.

Targeted Resources
❑ Learning with Documents booklet, *Tenement Factories*, p. 18 **L3**
❑ Presentation Pro CD-ROM, Chapter 13, Section 2 **L2**
❑ Exploring Primary Sources in U.S. History CD-ROM, *Wealth*, Andrew Carnegie **L3**

ASSESS/RETEACH

Monitor Progress
Assess students completed graphic organizers using the Section Reading Support Transparency. Review the answers to the Guided Reading and Review worksheet.

Assess
Use the Section 2 Quiz to evaluate student understanding of key concepts in this section.

Reteach
Assign students the section summary in the Guide to the Essentials.

Targeted Resources
❑ Section Reading Support Transparency **L1** **ELL**
❑ Guided Reading and Review booklet, p. 55 **L1**
❑ Section 2 Quiz, Unit 5/6 booklet, p. 7 **L1** **L2**
❑ Guide to the Essentials, p. 69 **L1** **L2**
❑ Social Studies Skills Tutor CD-ROM **L1**
❑ Guided Reading Audiotapes **ELL**
❑ Student Edition on Audio CD **ELL**

Homework _____

_____

Key
L1 Basic to Average   **L3** Average to Advanced
L2 For All Students   **ELL** English Language Learners

LESSON PLAN 13.3

Industrialization and Workers

🕐 *.5 Period, .25 Block*

Section Objectives

1. Find out about factors that led to a growing American workforce between 1860 and 1900.
2. Learn what factory work at the turn of the century was like.
3. Discover why it was sometimes necessary for entire families to work.

Local Standards

Vocabulary piecework • sweatshop • division of labor

FOCUS	**Targeted Resources**
Teach Key Concepts and Vocabulary Describe working life for an industrial worker in the late 1800s and early 1900s. **Build Background Knowledge** Help students compare a worker in a pre–Civil War blacksmithy to a worker in a Carnegie steel plant.	❏ Activating Prior Knowledge, TE p. 473 **L1**

INSTRUCT	**Targeted Resources**
Develop Understanding Millions of workers flocked to the new industries taking hold during this period. How did industrialization change employers, workers, and products? **Monitor Comprehension** Have students list the positive and negative effects of industrialization on workers.	❏ Learning Styles Lesson Plan booklet, p. 29 **L2** ❏ Learning with Documents booklet, *The Noble Face of Labor*, p. 52 **L3** ❏ Biography, Literature, and Comparing Primary Sources booklet, *The Stories of Horatio Alger*, p. 57 **L3** ❏ Presentation Pro CD-ROM, Chapter 13, Section 3 **L1**

ASSESS/RETEACH	**Targeted Resources**
Monitor Progress Assess students completed graphic organizers using the Section Reading Support Transparency. Rview the answers to the Guided Reading and Review worksheet. **Assess** Use the Section 3 Quiz to evaluate student understanding of key concepts in this section. **Reteach** Assign students the Guide to the Essentials.	❏ Section Reading Support Transparency **L1** **ELL** ❏ Guided Reading and Review booklet, p. 56 **L1** ❏ Section 3 Quiz, Unit 5/6 booklet, p. 8 **L1** **L2** ❏ Guide to the Essentials, p. 70 **L1** **L2** ❏ Social Studies Skills Tutor CD-ROM **L1** ❏ Guided Reading Audiotapes **ELL** ❏ Student Edition on Audio CD **ELL**

Homework _____

_____

Key
L1 Basic to Average   **L3** Average to Advanced
L2 For All Students   **ELL** English Language Learners

LESSON PLAN 13.4
The Great Strikes
⏱ *1 Period, .5 Block*

Section Objectives

1. Discover the impact of industrialism on the gulf between rich and poor.
2. Find out the goals of the early labor unions in the United States.
3. Learn why Eugene V. Debs formed the American Railway Union.
4. Study the causes and outcomes of the major strikes in the late 1800s.

Vocabulary socialism • craft union • collective bargaining • industrial union • scab • anarchist • Haymarket Riot • Homestead Strike • Pullman Strike

Local Standards

FOCUS

Teach Key Concepts and Vocabulary
How did workers try to improve their wages and working conditions in the late 1800s?

Build Background Knowledge
Explain that socialism, anarchism, and labor unions were different approaches to solving the problems of workers. How did socialism run counter to some American ideals?

Targeted Resources
❑ Activating Prior Knowledge, TE, p. 477 **L1**
❑ Sounds of an Era Audio CD, *"The Electric Light Quadrille"; "The Commonwealth of Toil"* **L3**

INSTRUCT

Develop Understanding
Discuss how labor unions attempted to address the problems of workers. What was public reaction to strikes? What pattern of events did the Pullman Strike set in motion?

Monitor Comprehension
Have students list the types of worker grievances that labor unions addressed.

Targeted Resources
❑ Biography, Literature, and Comparing Primary Sources booklet, *On Labor Unions*, p. 121; *Mary Kenney O'Sullivan*, p. 18 **L3**
❑ Presentation Pro CD-ROM, Chapter 13, Section 4 **L1**

ASSESS/RETEACH

Monitor Progress
Assess students completed graphic organizers using the Section Reading Support Transparency. Review the answers to the Guided Reading and Review worksheet.

Assess
Use the Section 4 Quiz to evaluate student understanding of key concepts in this section.

Reteach
Assign students the section summary in the Guide to the Essentials.

Targeted Resources
❑ Section Reading Support Transparency **L1 ELL**
❑ Guided Reading and Review booklet, p. 57 **L1**
❑ Section 4 Quiz, Units 5/6 booklet, p. 9 **L1 L2**
❑ Guide to the Essentials, p. 71 **L1 L2**
❑ Chapter Summary, Units 5/6 booklet, p. 3 **L1 ELL**
❑ GoOnline: PHSchool.com, Chapter 13 Self-Test, Web Code: mra-5135
❑ Chapter 13 Tests, Units 5/6 booklet, pp. 10, 13

Homework _____

_____

Key
L1 Basic to Average **L3** Average to Advanced
L2 For All Students **ELL** English Language Learners

LESSON PLAN 14.1

Moving West

🕐 *.5 Period, .25 Block*

Section Objectives

1. Learn about the kinds of conditions that lured people to migrate to the West.
2. Find out where western settlers came from.
3. Describe how the American frontier shifted westward.

Vocabulary push-pull factors • Pacific Railway Acts • Morrill Land-Grant Act • land speculator • Homestead Act • Exoduster

Local Standards

FOCUS	Targeted Resources

Teach Key Concepts and Vocabulary
What inspired people to head out West?

Build Background Knowledge
As students read, have them make note of who these setters were that migrated westward. How diverse was this population?

❑ Activating Prior Knowledge, TE, p. 488 **L1**
❑ Sounds of an Era Audio CD, *Cowboy Dan Deering* **L3**

INSTRUCT	Targeted Resources

Develop Understanding
Civil war veterans, immigrants, and former slaves moved west in search of fertile lands to call their own. Discuss how government incentives increased migration to the West.

Monitor Comprehension
Why did the federal government grant western lands to homesteaders, railroads, and state governments?

❑ Presentation Pro CD-ROM, Chapter 14, Section 1 **L1**
❑ Prentice Hall U.S. History Video Collection, Vol. 11, *Industrialization and Urbanization* **L2**

ASSESS/RETEACH	Targeted Resources

Monitor Progress
Assess students completed graphic organizers using the Section Reading Support Transparency. Review the answers to the Guided Reading and Review worksheet.

Assess
Use the Section 1 Quiz to evaluate student understanding of key concepts in this section.

Reteach
Assign students the section summary in the Guide to the Essentials.

❑ Section Reading Support Transparency **L1** **ELL**
❑ Guided Reading and Review booklet, p. 58 **L1**
❑ Section 1 Quiz, Unit 5/6 booklet, p. 15 **L1** **L2**
❑ Guide to the Essentials, p. 73 **L1** **L2**
❑ Social Studies Skills Tutor CD-ROM **L1**
❑ Guided Reading Audiotapes **ELL**
❑ Student Edition on Audio CD **ELL**

Homework _____

_____

Key
L1 Basic to Average   **L3** Average to Advanced
L2 For All Students   **ELL** English Language Learners

LESSON PLAN 14.2
Conflict With Native Americans
🕐 *1 Period, .5 Block*

Section Objectives

1. Study the factors that caused changes in the life of the Plains Indians.
2. Find out how government policies and battlefield challenges affected the Indian Wars.
3. Learn about changes that occurred in federal Indian policies by 1900.

Local Standards

Vocabulary Great Plains • nomad • reservation • Battle of Little Bighorn • Ghost Dance • Massacre at Wounded Knee • assimilation • Dawes Act • boomers • sooners

FOCUS

Teach Key Concepts and Vocabulary
What was the effect of westward expansion on Native Americans?
Build Background Knowledge
Explain that migrants and immigrants settled on land that had been home to Native Americans for many generations.

Targeted Resources

❏ Activating Prior Knowledge, TE, p. 491 **L1**
❏ Color Transparencies, Historical Maps, A25, A60 **L2**
❏ Historical Outline Map Book, *Indian Lands After 1850*, p. 55 **L1**
❏ Sounds of an Era Audio CD, *"It Is a Good Day to Die," Sioux War Song*; John G. Neihardt **L3**

INSTRUCT

Develop Understanding
Discuss the conflicting beliefs regarding land use and government held by Native Americans and settlers. What role did these differences play in the Indian Wars of the late 1800s?
Monitor Comprehension
How did attempts to change Native American culture contribute to their ruin? What were the results of the homesteading rush of 1898?

Targeted Resources

❏ Learning Styles Lesson Plan booklet, p. 30 **L2**
❏ Learning with Documents booklet, *Western Expansion into Native American Land*, p. 53 **L3**
❏ Biography, Literature, and Comparing Primary Sources booklet, *On Cultural Ties*, p. 125 **L3**
❏ Exploring Primary Sources in U.S. History CD-ROM, *Geronimo: His Own Story*, S. M. Barrett, ed. **L3**

ASSESS/RETEACH

Monitor Progress
Assess students completed graphic organizers using the Section Reading Support Transparency. Review the answers to the Guided Reading and Review worksheet.
Assess
Use the Section 2 Quiz to evaluate student understanding of key concepts in this section.
Reteach
Assign students the Guide to the Essentials.

Targeted Resources

❏ Section Reading Support Transparency **L1** **ELL**
❏ Guided Reading and Review booklet, p. 59 **L1**
❏ Section 2 Quiz, Units 5/6 booklet, p. 16 **L1** **L2**
❏ Guide to the Essentials, p. 74 **L1** **L2**

Homework _____

_____

Key
L1 Basic to Average   **L3** Average to Advanced
L2 For All Students   **ELL** English Language Learners

LESSON PLAN 14.3

Mining, Ranching, and Farming

1 Period, .5 Block

Section Objectives

1. Learn how mining spread in the West.
2. Find out what caused the western cattle boom.
3. See what life was like for a cowboy on the Chisholm Trail.
4. Discover how settlers overcame barriers in farming the plains.

Vocabulary pacer mining • long drive • homesteader • soddie • dry farming • bonanza farm • Turner thesis • stereotype

Local Standards

FOCUS

Teach Key Concepts and Vocabulary
Ask students how mining, ranching, and farming attracted both individual settlers and big businesses.

Build Background Knowledge
As students read, have them note the ways in which the farming, mining, and ranching industries changed in the second half of the nineteenth century.

Targeted Resources
❑ Activating Prior Knowledge, TE, p. 498 **L1**
❑ Color Transparencies, Historical Maps, A26 **L2**
❑ Historical Outline Map Book, *Opening the West*, p. 56 **L1**
❑ Sounds of an Era Audio CD, *"The Farmer Is the Man Who Feeds Them All"* **L3**

INSTRUCT

Develop Understanding
Discuss the role technology played in transforming the West. How did technology help the Great Plains farmers? Why did big business develop in the West?

Monitor Comprehension
Have students list some of the effects of the discovery of gold in California.

Targeted Resources
❑ Biography, Literature, and Comparing Primary Sources booklet, *The Californian's Tale*, p. 58; *Nat Love, Alias Deadwood Dick*, p. 19 **L3**
❑ Presentation Pro CD-ROM, Chapter 14, Section 3 **L1**
❑ Exploring Primary Sources in U.S. History CD-ROM, *Peary Reaches the North Pole*, Robert E. Peary **L3**

ASSESS/RETEACH

Monitor Progress
Assess students completed graphic organizers using the Section Reading Support Transparency. Review the answers to the Guided Reading and Review worksheet.

Assess
Use the Section 3 Quiz to evaluate student understanding of key concepts in this section.

Reteach
Assign students the Guide to the Essentials.

Targeted Resources
❑ Section Reading Support Transparency **L1** **ELL**
❑ Guided Reading and Review booklet, p. 60 **L1**
❑ Section 3 Quiz, Unit 5/6 booklet, p. 17 **L1** **L2**
❑ Guide to the Essentials, p. 75 **L1** **L2**
❑ Social Studies Skills Tutor CD-ROM **L1**

Homework _____

_____

Key
L1 Basic to Average   **L3** Average to Advanced
L2 For All Students   **ELL** English Language Learners

LESSON PLAN 14.4

Populism

🕐 *1 Period, .5 Block*

Section Objectives	Local Standards

Section Objectives

1. See why farmers complained about federal post–Civil War economic policies.
2. Find out how the government responded to organized protests by farmers.
3. Discover the Populists' key goals.
4. Understand the main point of William Jennings Bryan's Cross of Gold speech.
5. Learn about the legacy of Populism.

Vocabulary money supply • deflation • monetary policy • bimetallic standard • free silver • Bland-Allison Act • Sherman Silver Purchase Act • the Grange • Interstate Commerce Act • Populist • Cross of Gold speech

FOCUS

Teach Key Concepts and Vocabulary
What reforms did the Populists hope to institute?

Build Background Knowledge
Explain why farmers and industrialists were divided over the issues of tariffs.

Targeted Resources
❏ Activating Prior Knowledge, TE p. 507 **L1**
❏ Sounds of an Era Audio CD, *"Cross of Gold"* **L3**

INSTRUCT

Develop Understanding
Explain that as farmers' income declined, they began to join together in farmers' alliances. One political party formed out of these alliances was the Populist party, which demanded radical government reforms.

Monitor Comprehension
Have students list the four major planks in the Populist platform.

Targeted Resources
❏ Learning Styles Lesson Plan booklet, p. 31 **L2**
❏ Skills for Life booklet, p. 16 **L1**
❏ Learning with Documents booklet, William Jennings Bryan, *Cross of Gold Speech*, p. 83 **L3**
❏ Presentation Pro CD-ROM, Chapter 14, Section 4 **L1**

ASSESS/RETEACH

Monitor Progress
Assess students completed graphic organizers using the Section Reading Support Transparency. Review the answers to the Guided Reading and Review worksheet.

Assess
Use the Section 4 Quiz to evaluate student understanding of key concepts in this section.

Reteach
Assign students the section summary in the Guide to the Essentials.

Targeted Resources
❏ Section Reading Support Transparency **L1** **ELL**
❏ Guided Reading and Review booklet, p. 61 **L1**
❏ Section 4 Quiz, Units 5/6 booklet, p. 18 **L1** **L2**
❏ Guide to the Essentials, p. 76 **L1** **L2**
❏ Chapter Summary, Units 5/6 booklet, p. 14 **L1** **ELL**
❏ GoOnline: PHSchool.com, Chapter 14 Self-Test, Web Code: mra-5145
❏ Chapter 14 Tests, Unit 5/6 booklet, pp. 19, 22

Homework _____

_____

Key
L1 Basic to Average   **L3** Average to Advanced
L2 For All Students   **ELL** English Language Learners

LESSON PLAN 15.1

Politics in the Gilded Age

🕐 *1 Period, .5 Block*

Section Objectives

1. Find out how business influenced politics during the Gilded Age.
2. Learn the ways in which government reformed the spoils system and regulated railroads.
3. Discover the effect the transition from depression to prosperity had on politics in the 1890s.

Vocabulary Gilded Age • *laissez-faire* • subsidy • blue law • civil service • Pendleton Civil Service Act • rebate • *Munn v. Illinois*

Local Standards

FOCUS

Teach Key Concepts and Vocabulary
Ask students what role corruption and reform played in national politics in the late 1800s.
Build Background Knowledge
Review with students the reasons some Americans demanded reform.

Targeted Resources

❏ Activating Prior Knowledge, TE p. 520 **L1**
❏ Sounds of an Era Audio CD, *William McKinley* **L3**

INSTRUCT

Develop Understanding
Discuss how the cycle of depression of the early 1890s hurt Democrats and helped Republicans. Ask students to describe the efforts made by Presidents Hayes and Arthur to end the spoils system.
Monitor Comprehension
Why was it so difficult for the government to end the spoils system?

Targeted Resources

❏ Learning Styles Lesson Plan booklet, p. 32 **L2**
❏ Presentation Pro CD-ROM, Chapter 15, Section 1 **L1**
❏ Prentice Hall U.S. History Video Collection, Vol. 12, *Immigration and Cultural Change* **L2**

ASSESS/RETEACH

Monitor Progress
Assess students' completed graphic organizers using the Section Reading Support Transparency. Review the answers to the Guided Reading and Review worksheet.
Assess
Use the Section 1 Quiz to evaluate student understanding of key concepts in this section.
Reteach
Assign students the section summary in the Guide to the Essentials.

Targeted Resources

❏ Section Reading Support Transparency **L1** **ELL**
❏ Guided Reading and Review booklet, p. 62 **L1**
❏ Section 1 Quiz, Units 5/6 booklet, p. 26 **L1** **L2**
❏ Guide to the Essentials, p. 78 **L1** **L2**
❏ Social Studies Skills Tutor CD-ROM **L1**
❏ Guided Reading Audiotapes **ELL**
❏ Student Edition on Audio CD **ELL**

Homework _____

_____

Key
L1 Basic to Average   **L3** Average to Advanced
L2 For All Students   **ELL** English Language Learners

LESSON PLAN 15.2

People on the Move

🕐 *1 Period, .5 Block*

Section Objectives	**Local Standards**

1. Share the experiences of immigrants in the late 1800s and early 1900s.
2. Analyze the different challenges faced by immigrants from Europe, Asia, and Mexico.

Vocabulary pogrom • steerage • quarantine • ghetto • restrictive covenant • Chinese Exclusion Act • Gentlemen's Agreement • alien

FOCUS

Targeted Resources

Teach Key Concepts and Vocabulary
Ask students to describe the immigrant experience of the late 1800s and early 1900s.

Build Background Knowledge
As students read, have them consider the special problems encountered by Asian immigrants. How did Americans respond to Asian customs?

- ❏ Activating Prior Knowledge, TE p. 527 **L1**
- ❏ Sounds of an Era Audio CD, *Ellis Island Immigrants* **L3**

INSTRUCT

Targeted Resources

Develop Understanding
Ask students what drew immigrants to the United States. Discuss the different experiences of immigrants from Europe, Asia, and Mexico.

Monitor Comprehension
What difficulties did new immigrants face as they arrived in the United States?

- ❏ Learning Styles Lesson Plan booklet, p. 33 **L2**
- ❏ Learning with Documents booklet, *Passage to America*, p. 54 **L3**
- ❏ Biography, Literature, and Comparing Primary Sources booklet, *The Statue of Liberty*, p. 61; *On Cultural Ties*, p. 125 **L3**
- ❏ Presentation Pro CD-ROM, Chapter 15, Section 2 **L2**
- ❏ Exploring Primary Sources in U.S. History CD ROM, *Poems by Chinese Immigrants at Angel Island* **L3**

ASSESS/RETEACH

Targeted Resources

Monitor Progress
Assess students' completed graphic organizers using the Section Reading Support Transparency. Review the answers to the Guided Reading and Review worksheet.

Assess
Use the Section 2 Quiz to evaluate student understanding of key concepts in this section.

Reteach
Assign students the section summary in the Guide to the Essentials.

- ❏ Section Reading Support Transparency **L1** **ELL**
- ❏ Guided Reading and Review booklet, p. 63 **L1**
- ❏ Section 2 Quiz, Units 5/6 booklet, p. 27 **L1** **L2**
- ❏ Guide to the Essentials, p. 79 **L1** **L2**
- ❏ Social Studies Skills Tutor CD-ROM **L1**
- ❏ Guided Reading Audiotapes **ELL**
- ❏ Student Edition on Audio CD **ELL**

Homework _____

_____

Key
L1 Basic to Average   **L3** Average to Advanced
L2 For All Students   **ELL** English Language Learners

LESSON PLAN 15.3
The Challenge of the Cities
⏱ *1 Period, .5 Block*

Section Objectives

1. Find out why cities expanded in the late 1800s and early 1900s.
2. Review new developments that helped cities grow.
3. Learn how living conditions in cities changed.
4. State the results of city growth.

Vocabulary suburb • tenement • dumbbell tenement • political machine • graft

Local Standards

FOCUS

Teach Key Concepts and Vocabulary
How did cities expand and change in the late 1800s and early 1900s?

Build Background Knowledge
As students read, have them track the rise of the suburb and its role in the expansion of cities.

Targeted Resources
❏ Activating Prior Knowledge, TE p. 534 **L1**
❏ Sounds of an Era Audio CD, *"The Bowery,"* 1893 **L3**

INSTRUCT

Develop Understanding
Migration from the nation's rural areas to its cities added to their explosive growth. How did cities' burgeoning populations affect living conditions?

Monitor Comprehension
Have students create a chart showing the causes and effects of rapid city growth in the late 1800s and early 1900s.

Targeted Resources
❏ Skills for Life booklet, p. 17 **L1**
❏ Learning with Documents booklet, *New York Gangs*, p. 20 **L3**
❏ Biography, Literature, and Comparing Primary Sources booklet, *Thomas Nast*, p. 20 **L2**
❏ Presentation Pro CD-ROM, Chapter 15, Section 3 **L1**

ASSESS/RETEACH

Monitor Progress
Assess students' completed graphic organizers using the Section Reading Support Transparency. Review the answers to the Guided Reading and Review worksheet.

Assess
Use the Section 3 Quiz to evaluate student understanding of key concepts in this section.

Reteach
Assign students the section summary in the Guide to the Essentials.

Targeted Resources
❏ Section Reading Support Transparency **L1** **ELL**
❏ Guided Reading and Review booklet, p. 64 **L1**
❏ Section 3 Quiz, Units 5/6 booklet, p. 28 **L1** **L2**
❏ Guide to the Essentials, p. 80 **L1** **L2**
❏ Social Studies Skills Tutor CD-ROM **L1**
❏ Guided Reading Audiotapes **ELL**
❏ Student Edition on Audio CD **ELL**

Homework _____

_____

Key
L1 Basic to Average   **L3** Average to Advanced
L2 For All Students   **ELL** English Language Learners

LESSON PLAN 15.4

Ideas for Reform

🕐 .5 Period, .25 Block

Section Objectives

1. Study the ways in which different movements helped the needy.
2. Learn how and where sociology developed.
3. Examine efforts to control immigration and personal behavior in the late 1800s.

Local Standards

Vocabulary social gospel movement • settlement house • sociology • nativism • temperance movement • prohibition • vice

---

FOCUS

Teach Key Concepts and Vocabulary
How did reformers work to improve social, economic, and political conditions in the cities?

Build Background Knowledge
Discuss how the nativist and temperance movements linked immigration with the problems of cities.

Targeted Resources

❑ Activating Prior Knowledge, TE p. 541 **L1**

INSTRUCT

Develop Understanding
Discuss charitable approaches to reform, then compare them to more restrictive approaches. How did nativists and temperance movement reformers try to control immigration and individual behavior?

Monitor Comprehension
Have students list the efforts made by the different reform movements discussed in the section.

Targeted Resources

❑ Presentation Pro CD-ROM, Chapter 15, Section 4 **L1**

❑ Exploring Primary Sources in U.S. History CD-ROM, *Twenty Years at Hull House,* Jane Addams **L3**

ASSESS/RETEACH

Monitor Progress
Assess students' completed graphic organizers using the Section Reading Support Transparency. Review the answers to the Guided Reading and Review worksheet.

Assess
Use the Section 4 Quiz to evaluate student understanding of key concepts in this section.

Reteach
Assign students the section summary in the Guide to the Essentials.

Targeted Resources

❑ Section Reading Support Transparency **L1** **ELL**

❑ Guided Reading and Review booklet, p. 65 **L1**

❑ Section 4 Quiz, Units 5/6 booklet, p. 29 **L1** **L2**

❑ Guide to the Essentials, p. 81 **L1** **L2**

❑ Social Studies Skills Tutor CD-ROM **L1**

❑ Chapter Summary, Units 5/6 booklet, p. 25 **L1** **ELL**

❑ Go Online: PHSchool.com, Chapter 15 Self-Test, Web Code: mra-5155

❑ Chapter 15 Tests, Units 5/6 booklet, pp. 30, 33

Homework _____

_____

Key
L1 Basic to Average **L3** Average to Advanced
L2 For All Students **ELL** English Language Learners

LESSON PLAN 16.1

The Expansion of Education

🕐 *1 Period, .5 Block*

Section Objectives	**Local Standards**

Section Objectives

1. Learn how and why public schools expanded during the late 1800s.
2. Find out how opportunities for higher education increased after the Civil War.
3. Discover the views of Booker T. Washington and W. E. B. Du Bois regarding African American education.

Vocabulary literacy • assimilation • philanthropist • Niagara Movement

---

FOCUS

Teach Key Concepts and Vocabulary
Why did public schools expand during the late 1800s?

Build Background Knowledge
Explain that as the United States became more industrialized and urbanized after the Civil War, Americans needed to become more educated.

Targeted Resources
❑ Activating Prior Knowledge, TE p. 552 **L1**
❑ Sounds of an Era Audio CD, *Booker T. Washington; W. E. B. Du Bois* **L3**

INSTRUCT

Develop Understanding
Discuss the different educational experience of immigrants, African Americans, women, and people in rural areas.

Monitor Comprehension
How did Booker T. Washington's and W. E. B. Du Bois's approaches toward education for African Americans differ?

Targeted Resources
❑ Learning Styles Lesson Plan booklet, p. 21 **L2**
❑ Skills for Life booklet, p. 18 **L1**
❑ Learning with Documents booklet, *Pledge of Allegiance*, p. 84; *The Washington–Du Bois Debate*, p. 85 **L3**
❑ Presentation Pro CD-ROM, Chapter 16, Section 1 **L1**
❑ Prentice Hall U.S. History Video Collection, Vol. 11, *Immigration and Cultural Change* **L2**

ASSESS/RETEACH

Monitor Progress
Assess students' completed graphic organizers using the Section Reading Support Transparency. Review the answers to the Guided Reading and Review worksheet.

Assess
Use the Section 1 Quiz to evaluate student understanding of key concepts in this section.

Reteach
Assign students the section summary in the Guide to the Essentials.

Targeted Resources
❑ Section Reading Support Transparency **L1** **ELL**
❑ Guided Reading and Review booklet, p. 66 **L1**
❑ Section 1 Quiz, Units 5/6 booklet, p. 37 **L1** **L2**
❑ Guide to the Essentials, p. 83 **L1** **L2**
❑ Social Studies Skills Tutor CD-ROM **L1**
❑ Guided Reading Audiotapes **ELL**
❑ Student Edition on Audio CD **ELL**

Homework _____

_____

Key
L1 Basic to Average   **L3** Average to Advanced
L2 For All Students   **ELL** English Language Learners

LESSON PLAN 16.2
New Forms of Entertainment
🕐 .5 Period, .25 Block

Section Objectives

Local Standards

1. Discover the new kinds of performances and recreation that Americans enjoyed at the turn of the century.
2. Find out what people were reading for education and entertainment.
3. Learn how American music was changing.

Vocabulary vaudeville • yellow journalism • ragtime

FOCUS

Teach Key Concepts and Vocabulary
What new forms of entertainment emerged in the late 1800s?

Build Background Knowledge
Why were Americans looking for new ways to entertain themselves?

Targeted Resources

❏ Activating Prior Knowledge, TE p. 559 **L1**
❏ Sounds of an Era Audio CD, *"Maple Leaf Rag"; "Florida Rag"* **L3**

INSTRUCT

Develop Understanding
Discuss the new forms of entertainment of the late 1800s. Analyze the influence of African American music on popular culture.

Monitor Comprehension
Have students list the forms of entertainment that were popular in the United States between 1880 and 1915.

Targeted Resources

❏ Learning Styles Lesson Plan booklet, p. 34 **L2**
❏ Biography, Literature, and Comparing Primary Sources booklet, *George M. Cohan*, p. 21; *Around the World in 72 Days*, p. 62 **L3**
❏ Presentation Pro CD-ROM, Chapter 16, Section 2 **L1**

ASSESS/RETEACH

Monitor Progress
Assess students' completed graphic organizers using the Section Reading Support Transparency. Review the answers to the Guided Reading and Review worksheet.

Assess
Use the Section 2 Quiz to evaluate student understanding of key concepts in this section.

Reteach
Assign students the section summary in the Guide to the Essentials.

Targeted Resources

❏ Section Reading Support Transparency **L1** **ELL**
❏ Guided Reading and Review booklet, p. 67 **L1**
❏ Section 2 Quiz, Units 5/6 booklet, p. 38 **L1** **L2**
❏ Guide to the Essentials, p. 84 **L1** **L2**
❏ Social Studies Skills Tutor CD-ROM **L1**
❏ Guided Reading Audiotapes **ELL**
❏ Student Edition on Audio CD **ELL**

Homework _____

_____

Key
L1 Basic to Average   **L3** Average to Advanced
L2 For All Students   **ELL** English Language Learners

LESSON PLAN 16.3
The World of Jim Crow
.5 Period, .25 Block

Section Objectives

1. Probe the kinds of discrimination encountered by African Americans after Reconstruction.
2. Find out how African Americans resisted this discrimination.

Vocabulary poll tax • grandfather clause • segregation • Jim Crow • *Plessy* v. *Ferguson* • lynching • National Association for the Advancement of Colored People (NAACP)

Local Standards

FOCUS

Teach Key Concepts and Vocabulary
How were African Americans kept from achieving equality in the post-Reconstruction South?

Build Background Knowledge
Explain how and why some states used legal tactics to restrict African American voting rights.

Targeted Resources

❏ Activating Prior Knowledge, TE p. 564 **L1**

INSTRUCT

Develop Understanding
Discuss the tactics used by whites to prevent African Americans from exercising their full rights as citizens. How did African American community leaders respond to this discrimination?

Monitor Comprehension
How were some African Americans able to achieve success despite discrimination?

Targeted Resources

❏ Presentation Pro CD-ROM, Chapter 16, Section 3 **L1**

❏ American Heritage, My Brush with History, *Living Under Jim Crow,* Student Edition pp. 576–577, Videotape **L2**

ASSESS/RETEACH

Monitor Progress
Assess students' completed graphic organizers using the Section Reading Support Transparency. Review the answers to the Guided Reading and Review worksheet.

Assess
Use the Section 3 Quiz to evaluate student understanding of key concepts in this section.

Reteach
Assign students the section summary in the Guide to the Essentials.

Targeted Resources

❏ Section Reading Support Transparency **L1** **ELL**

❏ Guided Reading and Review booklet, p. 68 **L1**

❏ Section 3 Quiz, Units 5/6 booklet, p. 39 **L1** **L2**

❏ Guide to the Essentials, p. 85 **L1** **L2**

❏ Social Studies Skills Tutor CD-ROM **L1**

❏ Guided Reading Audiotapes **ELL**

❏ Student Edition on Audio CD **ELL**

Homework _____

_____

Key
L1 Basic to Average   **L3** Average to Advanced
L2 For All Students   **ELL** English Language Learners

LESSON PLAN 16.4

The Changing Roles of Women

🕐 .5 Period, .25 Block

Section Objectives

1. Examine the issues in the debate over women's equality.
2. Discover how women's work in the home changed at the turn of the century.
3. Learn how stores and catalogs served women's new role as consumers.
4. Find out about the kinds of work that women did outside the home.

Local Standards

Vocabulary department store • rural free delivery (RFD) • mail-order catalog

FOCUS	**Targeted Resources**

Teach Key Concepts and Vocabulary
How were women's lives changing in the late 1800s?

❏ Activating Prior Knowledge, TE p. 569 **L1**

Build Background Knowledge
As students read, have them list the demands of women's rights advocates.

INSTRUCT	**Targeted Resources**

Develop Understanding
Discuss the ways women's lives were changing in the late 1800s. Why were women's demands for more economic and political rights so controversial?

Monitor Comprehension
Have students list some of the changes in women's lives in the 1800s and early 1900s.

❏ Learning Styles Lesson Plan booklet, p. 35 **L2**
❏ Learning with Documents booklet, *The New Woman and the New Man*, p. 55 **L3**
❏ Biography, Literature, and Comparing Primary Sources booklet, *On the Woman Question*, p. 127 **L3**
❏ Presentation Pro CD-ROM, Chapter 16, Section 4 **L1**

ASSESS/RETEACH	**Targeted Resources**

Monitor Progress
Assess students' completed graphic organizers using the Section Reading Support Transparency. Review the answers to the Guided Reading and Review worksheet.

Assess
Use the Section 4 Quiz to evaluate student understanding of key concepts in this section.

Reteach
Assign students the section summary in the Guide to the Essentials.

❏ Section Reading Support Transparency **L1** **ELL**
❏ Guided Reading and Review booklet, p. 69 **L1**
❏ Section 4 Quiz, Unit 5/6 booklet, p. 40 **L1** **L2**
❏ Guide to the Essentials, p. 00 **L1** **L2**
❏ Chapter Summary, Units 5/6 booklet, p. 36 **L1** **ELL**
❏ GoOnline: PHSchool.com, Chapter 16 Self-Test, Web Code: mra-5165
❏ Chapter 16 Tests, Units 5/6 booklet, pp. 41, 44

Homework _____

_____

Key
L1 Basic to Average   **L3** Average to Advanced
L2 For All Students   **ELL** English Language Learners

LESSON PLAN 17.1
The Pressure to Expand
⏱ *.5 Period, .25 Block*

Section Objectives

1. Find out about the factors that led to the growth of imperialism around the world.
2. Learn about the ways in which the United States began to expand its interests abroad in the 1800s.
3. See the arguments made in favor of United States expansion in the 1890s.

Vocabulary imperialism• nationalism • annex • banana republic

Local Standards

FOCUS

Teach Key Concepts and Vocabulary
Why did the United States begin to expand its influence abroad in the late 1800s?

Build Background Knowledge
Why did business leaders put so much pressure on the U.S. government to support expansionist policies?

Targeted Resources

❑ Activating Prior Knowledge, TE p. 584 **L1**
❑ Color Transparencies, Time Lines, C5 **L2**
❑ Historical Outline Map Book, *The United States in the Caribbean, 1898–1917,* p. 58; *Central America and the Caribbean,* p. 81 **L1**

INSTRUCT

Develop Understanding
Discuss the worldwide growth of imperialism in the late 1800s. What role did economics play in U.S. territorial expansion? What other factors played a role in U.S. imperialism?

Monitor Comprehension
How did the United States respond to European imperialism in Asia and Africa?

Targeted Resources

❑ Presentation Pro CD-ROM, Chapter 17, Section 1 **L1**
❑ Prentice Hall U.S. History Video Collection, Vol. 15, *The United States and the World* **L2**

ASSESS/RETEACH

Monitor Progress
Assess students' completed graphic organizers using the Section Reading Support Transparency. Review the answers to the Guided Reading and Review worksheet.

Assess
Use the Section 1 Quiz to evaluate student understanding of key concepts in this section.

Reteach
Assign students the section summary in the Guide to the Essentials.

Targeted Resources

❑ Section Reading Support Transparency **L1** **ELL**
❑ Guided Reading and Review booklet, p. 70 **L1**
❑ Section 1 Quiz, Units 5/6 booklet, p. 52 **L1** **L2**
❑ Guide to the Essentials, p. 88 **L1** **L2**
❑ Social Studies Skills Tutor CD-ROM **L1**
❑ Guided Reading Audiotapes **ELL**
❑ Student Edition on Audio CD **ELL**

Homework _____
_____

Key
L1 Basic to Average **L3** Average to Advanced
L2 For All Students **ELL** English Language Learners

LESSON PLAN 17.2

The Spanish-American War

⏱ *1 Period, .5 Block*

Section Objectives

1. Read about United States activities in Latin America that set the stage for war with Spain.
2. Find out about events leading up to and following the Spanish-American War.
3. Discover challenges faced by the United States after the war.
4. Learn why the United States sought to gain influence in the Pacific.

Vocabulary arbitration • jingoism • Platt Amendment • sphere of influence • Open Door Policy

Local Standards

FOCUS

Teach Key Concepts and Vocabulary
What problems did the United States face as a world power?

Build Background Knowledge
Ask students what problems the United States faced as a new world power.

Targeted Resources

❑ Activating Prior Knowledge, TE p. 589 **L1**
❑ Color Transparencies, Historical Maps, A27, A30, A28 **L2**
❑ Historical Outline Map Book, *The Spanish-American War*, p. 57 **L1**
❑ Sounds of an Era Audio CD, *"Roosevelt's Charge"* and *"Teddy Roosevelt's Bugler"* **L3**

INSTRUCT

Develop Understanding
Review with students the steps leading to the Spanish-American War. Discuss how national pride and an aggressive foreign policy affected events in Chile, Cuba, the Philippines, and Hawaii in the late 1800s.

Monitor Comprehension
How did the United States' position among nations change as a result of the Spanish-American War?

Targeted Resources

❑ Learning Styles Lesson Plan booklet, p. 36 **L2**
❑ Skills for Life booklet, p. 19 **L1**
❑ Learning with Documents booklet, *Wartime Propaganda*, p. 56 **L3**
❑ Biography, Literature, and Comparing Primary Sources booklet, *Walter Reed*, p. 22 **L3**
❑ Presentation Pro CD-ROM, Chapter 17, Section 2 **L1**

ASSESS/RETEACH

Monitor Progress
Assess students' completed graphic organizers using the Section Reading Support Transparency.

Assess
Use the Section 2 Quiz to evaluate student understanding of key concepts in this section.

Reteach
Assign students the Guide to the Essentials.

Targeted Resources

❑ Section Reading Support Transparency **L1** **ELL**
❑ Guided Reading and Review booklet, p. 71 **L1**
❑ Section 2 Quiz, Units 5/6 booklet, p. 53 **L1** **L2**
❑ Guide to the Essentials, p. 89 **L1** **L2**
❑ Social Studies Skills Tutor CD-ROM **L1**
❑ Student Edition on Audio CD **ELL**

Homework _____
_____

Key
L1 Basic to Average   **L3** Average to Advanced
L2 For All Students   **ELL** English Language Learners

LESSON PLAN 17.3

A New Foreign Policy

🕐 *1 Period, .5 Block*

Section Objectives

1. Find out why the United States wanted to build the Panama Canal.
2. Learn about the goals of Roosevelt's "big stick" diplomacy.
3. Discover some ways in which the foreign policies of Presidents Taft and Wilson differed from those of President Roosevelt.

Vocabulary concession • Roosevelt Corollary • dollar diplomacy

Local Standards

| **FOCUS** | **Targeted Resources** |

Teach Key Concepts and Vocabulary
How did foreign policy develop in the early 1900s?

Build Background Knowledge
As students read, have them compare Roosevelt's foreign policy dealings in Latin America with those in Asia.

Targeted Resources

❏ Activating Prior Knowledge, TE p. 598 **L1**
❏ Color Transparencies; Historical Maps, A29 **L2**
❏ Historical Outline Map Book, *The Panama Canal*, p. 59 **L1**
❏ Sounds of an Era Audio CD, *William Howard Taft* **L3**

INSTRUCT

Develop Understanding
Discuss how Roosevelt's approach to foreign policy differed from Taft's. How would you characterize Wilson's foreign policy?

Monitor Comprehension
Why did the United States want to build the Panama Canal? How did Roosevelt acquire the necessary treaty to build the canal?

Targeted Resources

❏ Learning with Documents booklet, *Theodore Roosevelt, the Strenuous Life*, p. 85 **L3**
❏ Biography, Literature, and Comparing Primary Sources booklet, *You're All Right, Teddy*, p. 63 **L3**
❏ Presentation Pro CD-ROM, Chapter 17, Section 3 **L1**
❏ Exploring Primary Sources in U.S. History CD-ROM, *Roosevelt Corollary* **L3**

ASSESS/RETEACH

Monitor Progress
Assess students' completed graphic organizers using the Section Reading Support Transparency. Review the answers to the Guided Reading and Review worksheet.

Assess
Use the Section 3 Quiz to evaluate student understanding of key concepts in this section.

Reteach
Assign students the section summary in the Guide to the Essentials.

Targeted Resources

❏ Section Reading Support Transparency **L1** **ELL**
❏ Guided Reading and Review booklet, p. 72 **L1**
❏ Section 3 Quiz, Units 5/6 booklet, p. 54 **L1** **L2**
❏ Guide to the Essentials, p. 00 **L1** **L2**
❏ Social Studies Skills Tutor CD-ROM **L1**
❏ Guided Reading Audiotapes **ELL**
❏ Student Edition on Audio CD **ELL**

Homework _____

_____

Key
L1 Basic to Average   **L3** Average to Advanced
L2 For All Students   **ELL** English Language Learners

LESSON PLAN 17.4

Debating America's New Role

⏱ *.5 Period, .25 Block*

Section Objectives

1. Examine the main arguments raised by the anti-imperialists.
2. See why imperialism appealed to many Americans.
3. Find out how American imperialism was viewed from abroad.

Local Standards

Vocabulary racism • compulsory • Great White Fleet

FOCUS

Teach Key Concepts and Vocabulary
On what grounds did some Americans oppose imperialism?

Build Background Knowledge
Explain to students that anti-imperialists were fighting against Americans' spirited frontier mentality.

Targeted Resources
❑ Activating Prior Knowledge, TE p. 604 **L1**

INSTRUCT

Develop Understanding
Discuss with students the reasons professionals, southern Democrats, labor leaders, and African Americans opposed imperialism. What role did racism play in the arguments of both imperialists and anti-imperialists?

Monitor Comprehension
Have students list the arguments anti-imperialists used to support their case.

Targeted Resources
❑ Learning Styles Lesson Plan booklet, p. 37 **L2**
❑ Biography, Literature, and Comparing Primary Sources booklet, *On the Race for Empire*, p. 129 **L3**
❑ Presentation Pro CD-ROM, Chapter 17, Section 4 **L1**

ASSESS/RETEACH

Monitor Progress
Assess students' completed graphic organizers using the Section Reading Support Transparency. Review the answers to the Guided Reading and Review worksheet.

Assess
Use the Section 4 Quiz to evaluate student understanding of key concepts in this section.

Reteach
Assign students the section summary in the Guide to the Essentials.

Targeted Resources
❑ Section Reading Support Transparency **L1** **ELL**
❑ Guided Reading and Review booklet, p. 73 **L1**
❑ Section 4 Quiz, Units 5/6 booklet, p. 55 **L1** **L2**
❑ Guide to the Essentials, p. 91 **L1** **L2**
❑ Social Studies Skills Tutor CD-ROM **L1**
❑ Chapter Summary, Units 5/6 booklet, p. 51 **L1** **ELL**
❑ GoOnline: PHSchool.com, Chapter 17 Self-Test, Web Code: mra-6175
❑ Chapter 17 Tests, Units 5/6 booklet, pp. 56, 59

Homework _____
_____

Key
L1 Basic to Average   **L3** Average to Advanced
L2 For All Students   **ELL** English Language Learners

LESSON PLAN 18.1
The Origins of Progressivism
⏱ *.5 Period, .25 Block*

Section Objectives

1. Learn the key goals of Progressives.
2. Find out how the ideas of progressive writers helped inspire new reform movements.
3. Discover which reform organizations and which women reformers took up progressive causes.
4. Understand why progressive reforms met with resistance.

Vocabulary Progressive Era • muckraker • injunction

Local Standards

FOCUS	Targeted Resources

Teach Key Concepts and Vocabulary
Ask students to identify aspects of American life that Progressives hoped to reform.

Build Background Knowledge
Remind students that rapid industrialization, immigration, and urbanization in the late 1800s had created a new set of problems that Progressives wanted to solve.

❏ Activating Prior Knowledge, TE p. 614 **L1**
❏ Sounds of an Era Audio CD, *Upton Sinclair Interview* **L2**

INSTRUCT	Targeted Resources

Develop Understanding
Review the goals of the Populists, including increased circulation of money, unlimited minting of silver, an income tax, and an eight-hour work day. Compare and contrast these goals with those of the Progressives.

Monitor Comprehension
Have students discuss how progressive writers, such as Upton Sinclair, and progressive organizations, such as the National Consumers' League, advanced the cause of reform.

❏ Learning Styles Lesson Plan booklet, p. 38 **L2**
❏ Skills for Life booklet, p. 20 **L1**
❏ Biography, Literature, and Comparing Primary Sources booklet, *Horrors of the Meat-Packing Industry*, p. 64; *Ida Tarbell*, p. 23 **L3**
❏ Presentation Pro CD-ROM, Chapter 18, Section 1 **L1**
❏ Exploring Primary Sources in U.S. History CD-ROM, *The Jungle*, Upton Sinclair **L3**
❏ Prentice Hall U.S. History Video Collection, Vol. 14, *The Progressive Movement* **L2**

ASSESS/RETEACH	Targeted Resources

Monitor Progress
Assess students' completed graphic organizers using the Section Reading Support Transparency.

Assess
Use the Section 1 Quiz to evaluate student understanding of key concepts in this section.

Reteach
Assign students the Guide to the Essentials.

Homework _____

_____

❏ Section Reading Support Transparencies **L1** **ELL**
❏ Guided Reading and Review booklet, p. 74 **L1**
❏ Section 1 Quiz, Units 5/6 booklet, p. 63 **L1** **L2**
❏ Guide to the Essentials, p. 93 **L1** **L2**
❏ Guided Reading Audiotapes **ELL**
❏ Student Edition on Audio CD **ELL**

Key
L1 Basic to Average   **L3** Average to Advanced
L2 For All Students   **ELL** English Language Learners

LESSON PLAN 18.2
Progressive Legislation
⏱ *1 Period, .5 Block*

Section Objectives

1. Read about how Progressives wished to expand the role of government.
2. Discover the municipal and state reforms achieved by Progressives.
3. Learn what federal reforms Theodore Roosevelt championed as President.

Vocabulary social welfare program • municipal • home rule • direct primary • initiative • referendum • recall • holding company

Local Standards

FOCUS

Teach Key Concepts and Vocabulary
Ask students to list the municipal, state, and federal reform bills that Progressives passed and explain the purpose of each.

Build Background Knowledge
Explain that Progressives wanted government to regulate business and do more to help Americans in need, but they also wanted to reform the government.

Targeted Resources
❏ Activating Prior Knowledge, TE p. 621 **L1**

INSTRUCT

Develop Understanding
Have students discuss how municipal activists and politicians at the local, state, and federal level introduced reforms that affected business, social conditions, and government itself.

Monitor Comprehension
Ask students how voters gained power during the Progressive Era.

Targeted Resources
❏ Learning with Documents booklet, *The Shame of the People*, p. 57 **L3**
❏ Presentation Pro CD-ROM, Chapter 18, Section 2 **L1**

ASSESS/RETEACH

Monitor Progress
Assess students' completed graphic organizers using the Section Reading Support Transparency. Review the answers to the Guided Reading and Review worksheet.

Assess
Use the Section 2 Quiz to evaluate student understanding of key concepts in this section.

Reteach
Assign students the section summary in the Guide to the Essentials.

Targeted Resources
❏ Section Reading Support Transparencies **L1** **ELL**
❏ Guided Reading and Review booklet, p. 75 **L1**
❏ Section 2 Quiz, Units 5/6 booklet, p. 64 **L1** **L2**
❏ Guide to the Essentials, p. 94 **L1** **L2**
❏ Guided Reading Audiotapes **ELL**
❏ Student Edition on Audio CD **ELL**

Homework _____
_____

Key
L1 Basic to Average   **L3** Average to Advanced
L2 For All Students   **ELL** English Language Learners

LESSON PLAN 18.3

Progressivism Under Taft and Wilson

⏱ *1 Period, .5 Block*

Section Objectives

Local Standards

1. Study the political conflicts that marked the presidency of William Howard Taft.
2. Find out who contended in the election of 1912 and learn the outcome of that election.
3. Learn about the major policies that President Woodrow Wilson put into place.
4. Discover the limitations placed on the achievements of progressivism

Vocabulary conservationist • New Nationalism • Bull Moose Party • Clayton Antitrust Act • Federal Trade Commission (FTC) • Federal Reserve System

FOCUS

Teach Key Concepts and Vocabulary
Ask students to explain why groups linked with the progressive movement established their own political party.

Build Background Knowledge
Explain to students that actions Theodore Roosevelt took as President to regulate business and improve public health and the environment made him a hero to many Progressives.

Targeted Resources

❏ Activating Prior Knowledge, TE p. 628 **L1**
❏ Color Transparencies, American Photo, F6 **L2**
❏ Sounds of an Era Audio CD, *Teddy Roosevelt, 1912; Woodrow Wilson, 1912* **L2**

INSTRUCT

Develop Understanding
Discuss how the relationship between Theodore Roosevelt and William Howard Taft changed over the years and how their differences helped Woodrow Wilson gain the presidency.

Monitor Comprehension
Ask students to explain how Wilson's policies as President increased the power of the federal government.

Targeted Resources

❏ Presentation Pro CD-ROM, Chapter 18, Section 3 **L1**

ASSESS/RETEACH

Monitor Progress
Assess students' completed graphic organizers using the Section Reading Support Transparency.

Assess
Use the Section 3 Quiz to evaluate student understanding of key concepts in this section.

Reteach
Assign students the Guide to the Essentials.

Targeted Resources

❏ Section Reading Support Transparencies **L1** **ELL**
❏ Guided Reading and Review booklet, p. 76 **L1**
❏ Section 3 Quiz, Units 5/6 booklet, p. 65 **L1** **L2**
❏ Guide to the Essentials, p. 95 **L1** **L2**
❏ Guided Reading Audiotapes **ELL**
❏ Student Edition on Audio CD **ELL**

Homework _____
_____

Key
L1 Basic to Average   **L3** Average to Advanced
L2 For All Students   **ELL** English Language Learners

LESSON PLAN 18.4
Suffrage at Last
🕐 .5 Period, .25 Block

Section Objectives

Local Standards

1. Learn the ways in which Susan B. Anthony and Elizabeth Cady Stanton formed a "bridge" to the twentieth-century suffrage effort.
2. Discover two main strategies pursued by suffrage leaders.
3. Read about the status of the suffrage movement by the turn of the century.
4. Find out why a new generation of leaders was needed in the suffrage effort.
5. Study the factors that led to a final victory for suffrage.

Vocabulary civil disobedience • National American Woman Suffrage Association (NAWSA) • Congressional Union (CU)

FOCUS

Targeted Resources

Teach Key Concepts and Vocabulary
Ask students to explain the difference between civil disobedience and typical criminal behavior.

Build Background Knowledge
Remind students that suffragists faced strong opposition from many Americans who did not believe in giving women the right to vote.

❏ Activating Prior Knowledge, TE p. 635 **L1**
❏ Color Transparencies, Political Cartoons, B11 **L2**
❏ Sounds of an Era Audio CD, *Carrie Chapman Catt* **L2**

INSTRUCT

Targeted Resources

Develop Understanding
Discuss with students how members of the women's suffrage movement used civil disobedience and other strategies to press for the right to vote.

Monitor Comprehension
Ask students why a split developed in the suffrage movement.

❏ Learning Styles Lesson Plans booklet, pp. 38–39 **L2**
❏ Biography, Literature, and Comparing Primary Sources booklet, *On the Nineteenth Amendment*, p. 131 **L3**
❏ Exploring Primary Sources in U.S. History CD-ROM, *Are Not the Women Half the Nation?* **L3**

ASSESS/RETEACH

Targeted Resources

Monitor Progress
Assess students' completed graphic organizers using the Section Reading Support Transparency.

Assess
Use the Section 4 Quiz to evaluate student understanding of key concepts in this section.

Reteach
Assign students the Guide to the Essentials.

❏ Section Reading Support Transparency **L1 ELL**
❏ Guided Reading and Review booklet, p. 77 **L1**
❏ Section 4 Quiz, Units 5/6 booklet, p. 66 **L1 L2**
❏ Guide to the Essentials, p. 96 **L1 L2**
❏ GoOnline: PHSchool.com, Chapter 18 Self-Test, Web Code: mra-6185
❏ Chapter 18 Tests, Units 5/6 booklet, pp. 67, 70

Homework _____

_____

Key
L1 Basic to Average   **L3** Average to Advanced
L2 For All Students   **ELL** English Language Learners

LESSON PLAN 19.1
The Road to War
🕐 .5 Period, .25 Block

Section Objectives

1. Identify the main causes of World War I.
2. Understand how the conflict expanded to draw in much of Europe.
3. Analyze how the United States responded to the war in Europe.

Vocabulary militarism • mobilization • Central Powers • Allies • stalemate • autocrat • propaganda

FOCUS	**Targeted Resources**
Teach Key Concepts and Vocabulary Ask students to define the word *neutral* and to think of a situation in which they remained neutral. Why did they want to remain neutral? **Build Background Knowledge** Explain that when World War I first broke out, most Americans wished to remain neutral.	❑ Activating Prior Knowledge, TE p. 646 **L1** ❑ Color Transparencies, Historical Maps, A31, A32, A33, A34; *Time Lines*, C6 **L2** ❑ Historical Outline Map Book, *Europe in World War I*, p. 60 **L1** ❑ Sounds of an Era Audio CD *"Castle Walk,"* 1914 **L3**

INSTRUCT	**Targeted Resources**
Develop Understanding Discuss the underlying causes of the war including imperialism, militarism, and nationalism. Ask students to explain why the system of secret European alliances failed to prevent war. **Monitor Comprehension** Ask students to consider how new weapons changed the way soldiers fought.	❑ Learning Styles Lesson Plans booklet, p. 40 **L2** ❑ Learning with Documents booklet, *Thoughts on the War*, p. 24 **L3** ❑ Skills for Life booklet p. 21 **L1** ❑ Biography, Literature, and Comparing Primary Sources booklet, *A War Song*, p. 66 **L3** ❑ Presentation Pro CD-ROM, Chapter 19, Section 1 **L1** ❑ Prentice Hall U.S. History Video Collection, Vol. 16, *The Great War* **L2**

ASSESS/RETEACH	**Targeted Resources**
Monitor Progress Assess students' completed graphic organizers using the Section Reading Support Transparency. Review the answers to the Guided Reading and Review worksheet. **Assess** Use the Section 1 Quiz to evaluate student understanding of key concepts in this section. **Reteach** Assign students the section summary in the Guide to the Essentials.	❑ Section Reading Support Transparency **L1** **ELL** ❑ Guided Reading and Review booklet, p. 78 **L1** ❑ Section 1 Quiz, Units 5/6 booklet, p. 74 **L1** **L2** ❑ Guide to the Essentials, p. 98 **L1** **L2** ❑ Social Studies Skills Tutor CD-ROM **L1** **L2** ❑ Guided Reading Audiotapes **ELL**

Homework _____

_____

Key
L1 Basic to Average   **L3** Average to Advanced
L2 For All Students   **ELL** English Language Learners

LESSON PLAN 19.2

The United States Declares War

⏱ .5 Period, .25 Block

Section Objectives
1. Discover how Germany's use of submarines affected the war.
2. Find out the steps the United States took toward war in early 1917.

Local Standards

Vocabulary U-boat • Sussex pledge • Zimmermann note • Russian Revolution

FOCUS

Teach Key Concepts and Vocabulary
Ask students to explain why the United States finally declared war on the Central Powers in 1917.

Build Background Knowledge
Explain that from 1915 to 1917 relations between the United States and Germany deteriorated to the point of unrestricted submarine warfare by Germany against American vessels.

Targeted Resources

❑ Activating Prior Knowledge, TE p. 653 **L1**

❑ Sounds of the Era Audio CD, *"I Didn't Raise My Boy to be a Soldier,"* 1916 **L3**

INSTRUCT

Develop Understanding
Discuss why Germany's use of submarines caused outrage among Americans.

Monitor Comprehension
Have students discuss the roles of the Sussex pledge, the Zimmerman note, the Russian Revolution, British propaganda, and idealism in the American decision to enter the war.

Targeted Resources

❑ Biography, Literature, and Comparing Primary Sources booklet, *Jeanette Rankin*, p. 66 **L3**

❑ Presentation Pro CD-ROM, Chapter 19, Section 2 **L1**

❑ Exploring Primary Source in U.S. History CD-ROM, *The Zimmerman Telegram* **L3**

ASSESS/RETEACH

Monitor Progress
Assess students' completed graphic organizers using the Section Reading Support Transparency. Review the answers to the Guided Reading and Review worksheet.

Assess
Use the Section 2 Quiz to evaluate student understanding of key concepts in this section.

Reteach
Assign students the section summary in the Guide to the Essentials.

Targeted Resources

❑ Section Reading Support Transparency **L1** **ELL**

❑ Guided Reading and Review booklet, p. 79 **L1**

❑ Section 2 Quiz, Units 5/6 booklet, p. 75 **L1** **L2**

❑ Guide to the Essentials, p. 98 **L1** **L2**

❑ Guided Reading Audiotapes **ELL**

Homework _____

_____

Key
L1 Basic to Average **L3** Average to Advanced
L2 For All Students **ELL** English Language Learners

LESSON PLAN 19.3

Americans on the European Front

⏱ *1 Period, .5 Block*

Section Objectives

1. Analyze the preparations of the United States for World War I.
2. Study the ways in which the American troops helped turn the tide of the war.
3. Learn about conditions in Europe and the United States at the end of the war.

Local Standards _____

Vocabulary Selective Service Act • American Expeditionary Force (AEF) • convoy • zeppelin • armistice • genocide

---

FOCUS

Teach Key Concepts and Vocabulary
Ask students to describe how American involvement affected the war.

Build Background Knowledge
Remind students that initially Congress sent the Allies naval support, supplies, arms, and money in the form of loans because the American army was not prepared to go to Europe in large numbers.

Targeted Resources
❏ Activating Prior Knowledge, TE p. 657 **L1**
❏ Historical Outline Map book, *The Western Front*, p. 61
❏ Sounds of the Era Audio CD, *General Pershing*, 1917
❏ American Heritage, My Brush With History, *A Flyer on the Edge,* Student Edition pp. 676–677, Videotape **L3**

INSTRUCT

Develop Understanding
Ask students to list the steps required to create an army large enough to fight a war on the scale of World War I.

Monitor Comprehension
Ask students to locate on a map the major battles of the war involving Americans and to describe their outcomes. What role did American troops play in ending the war?

Targeted Resources
❏ Color Transparencies, *The Way It Works*, H15, H16 **L2**
❏ Presentation Pro CD-ROM, Chapter 19, Section 3 **L1**
❏ Exploring Primary Source in U.S. History CD-ROM, *Diary of a World War I Ambulance Driver,* William Stevenson **L3**

ASSESS/RETEACH

Monitor Progress
Assess students' completed graphic organizers using the Section Reading Support Transparency. Review the answers to the Guided Reading and Review worksheet.

Assess
Use the Section 3 Quiz to evaluate student understanding of key concepts in this section.

Reteach
Assign students the section summary in the Guide to the Essentials.

Targeted Resources
❏ Section Reading Support Transparency **L1 ELL**
❏ Guided Reading and Review booklet, p. 80 **L1**
❏ Section 3 Quiz, Units 5/6 booklet, p. 76 **L1 L2**
❏ Guide to the Essentials, p. 100 **L1 L2**
❏ Guided Reading Audiotape **ELL**

Homework _____

_____

Key
L1 Basic to Average   **L3** Average to Advanced
L2 For All Students   **ELL** English Language Learners

LESSON PLAN 19.4

Americans on the Home Front

⏱ *.5 Period, .25 Block*

Section Objectives

1. Learn about the steps the government took to finance the war and manage the economy.
2. Describe how the government enforced loyalty to the war effort.
3. Find out how the war changed the lives of Americans on the home front.

Vocabulary Liberty Bond • price controls • rationing • daylight saving time • sedition • vigilante

Local Standards

FOCUS

Teach Key Concepts and Vocabulary
Ask students what is meant by the term home front. Discuss with students the expanded role of the federal government during war time, including greater control of the economy and restricting civil liberties.

Build Background Knowledge
Ask students how the war lead to the suppression of civil liberties.

Targeted Resources
❏ Activating Prior Knowledge, TE p. 664 **L1**
❏ Sounds of the Era Audio CD, *"Over There,"* 1917 **L3**

INSTRUCT

Develop Understanding
Have students list changes in American life caused by the war and then categorize the changes.

Monitor Comprehension
Ask discuss students to discuss the roles of the War Industries Board and the War Labor Policies Board. Why did business and labor cooperate with these boards?

Targeted Resources
❏ Learning with Documents booklet, *Women's Roles in World War I*, p. 58
❏ Presentation Pro CD-ROM, Chapter 19, Section 4 **L1**

ASSESS/RETEACH

Monitor Progress
Assess students' completed graphic organizers using the Section Reading Support Transparency. Review the answers to the Guided Reading and Review worksheet.

Assess
Use the Section 4 Quiz to evaluate student understanding of key concepts in this section.

Reteach
Assign students the section summary in the Guide to the Essentials.

Targeted Resources
❏ Section Reading Support Transparency **L1** **ELL**
❏ Guided Reading and Review booklet, p. 81 **L1**
❏ Section 4 Quiz, Units 5/6 booklet, p. 77 **L1** **L2**
❏ Guide to the Essentials, p. 101 **L1** **L2**
❏ Guided Reading Audiotapes **ELL**

Homework _____

_____

Key
L1 Basic to Average   **L3** Average to Advanced
L2 For All Students   **ELL** English Language Learners

LESSON PLAN 19.5

Global Peacemaker

🕐 *1 Period, .5 Block*

Section Objectives

1. Discover the expectations that Wilson and the Allies brought to the Paris peace conference.
2. Learn about the important provisions of the peace treaty.
3. Find out how the federal government and ordinary Americans reacted to the end of the war.

Local Standards

Vocabulary Fourteen Points • self-determination • spoils • League of Nations • reparations • Versailles Treaty

FOCUS

Teach Key Concepts and Vocabulary
Ask students to discuss the contents of Wilson's Fourteen Points.

Build Background Knowledge
Ask students to list the main provisions of the Versailles Treaty. Ask them to color an outline map of Europe after World War I.

Targeted Resources
- ❑ Activating Prior Knowledge, TE p. 669 **L1**
- ❑ Historical Outline Map Book, *Europe After World War I*, p. 62 **L1**

INSTRUCT

Develop Understanding
Ask students how the loss of Republican support hurt Wilson's efforts to get Congress to ratify the Versailles Treaty.

Monitor Comprehension
Discuss why harsh conditions were imposed on Germany after the war and why many Americans had trouble adjusting to life after the war.

Targeted Resources
- ❑ Learning Styles Lesson Plans, p. 41 **L2**
- ❑ Learning with Documents booklet, Woodrow Wilson, *The Fourteen Points*, p. 86 **L3**
- ❑ Biography, Literature, and Comparing Primary Sources booklet, *On the League of Nations*, p. 133 **L3**
- ❑ Exploring Primary Sources in U.S. History CD-ROM, *The Fourteen Points* **L3**

ASSESS/RETEACH

Monitor Progress
Assess students' completed graphic organizers using the Section Reading Support Transparency. Review the answers to the Guided Reading and Review worksheet.

Assess
Use the Section 5 Quiz to evaluate student understanding of key concepts in this section.

Reteach
Assign students the section summary in the Guide to the Essentials.

Targeted Resources
- ❑ Section Reading Support Transparency **L1 ELL**
- ❑ Guided Reading and Review booklet, p. 82 **L1**
- ❑ Section 5 Quiz, Units 5/6 booklet, p. 78 **L1 L2**
- ❑ Guide to the Essentials, p. 102 **L1 L2**
- ❑ Chapter Summary, Units 5/6 booklet, p. 73 **L1 ELL**
- ❑ GoOnline: PHSchool.com, Chapter 19 Self-Test, Web Code: mra-6196
- ❑ Chapter 19 Tests, Units 5/6 booklet, pp. 79, 82

Homework _____

_____

Key
L1 Basic to Average   **L3** Average to Advanced
L2 For All Students   **ELL** English Language Learners

LESSON PLAN 20.1

Society in the 1920s

⏱ *1 Period, .5 Block*

Section Objectives

1. Learn how women's roles changed in the 1920s.
2. Find out how the nation's cities and suburbs were affected by Americans on the move from rural areas.
3. Read about America's heroes of the 1920s, and come to see the reasons for their popularity.

Vocabulary flapper • demographics • barrio

Local Standards

FOCUS

Teach Key Concepts and Vocabulary
Ask students to identify the new social and demographic trends that affected society in the 1920s.

Build Background Knowledge
Remind students that women stood at the center of a revolution in manners and morals that swept American society after World War I.

Targeted Resources

❏ Activating Prior Knowledge, TE p. 684 **L1**

❏ Color Transparencies, Fine Art, E17; American Diversity, G19 **L2**

❏ Sounds of an Era Audio CD, *"Have You Seen Rosie's Sister?"* 1925; *Charles Lindbergh,* 1927 **L3**

INSTRUCT

Develop Understanding
Discuss how women's changing role and increased migration affected America in the 1920s.

Monitor Comprehension
Ask students to explain how heroes of aviation and of sports met Americans' needs in the 1920s.

Targeted Resources

❏ Exploring Primary Sources in U.S. History CD-ROM, *A Flapper's Appeal to Parents,* Ellen Welles Page; *Charles Lindbergh's Transatlantic Flight, The Japan Times; The Report of the Committee on Recent Economic Changes* **L3**

❏ Prentice Hall U.S. History Video Collection, Vol. 17, *The Roaring Twenties*

ASSESS/RETEACH

Monitor Progress
Assess students' completed graphic organizers using the Section Reading Support Transparency. Review the answers to the Guided Reading and Review worksheet.

Assess
Use the Section 1 Quiz to evaluate student understanding of key concepts in this section.

Reteach
Assign students the section summary in the Guide to the Essentials.

Targeted Resources

❏ Section Reading Support Transparencies **L1** **ELL**

❏ Guided Reading and Review booklet, p. 83 **L1**

❏ Section 1 Quiz, Units 7/8 booklet, p. 4 **L1** **L2**

❏ Guide to the Essentials, p. 104 **L1** **L2**

Homework _____

_____

Key

L1 Basic to Average   **L3** Average to Advanced
L2 For All Students   **ELL** English Language Learners

LESSON PLAN 20.2

Section 2 Mass Media and the Jazz Age

⊙ *1 Period, .5 Block*

Section Objectives

1. See how the mass media helped create common cultural experiences.
2. Realize why the decade of the 1920s was called the Jazz Age, and learn how the jazz spirit affected the arts.
3. Discover how the writers of the Lost Generation responded to popular culture.
4. Find out about some of the subjects explored by the writers of the Harlem Renaissance.

Local Standards

Vocabulary mass media • Jazz Age • Lost Generation • Harlem Renaissance

FOCUS

Teach Key Concepts and Vocabulary
Ask students to define the term *mass media* and discuss why the rise of the mass media helped unify the country culturally.

Build Background Knowledge
Explain that before 1900, American culture varied from place to place. People read a local newspaper, entertained themselves with games or other family activities, and attended live plays or musical events where available.

Targeted Resources

❑ Activating Prior Knowledge, TE p. 691 **L1**
❑ Sounds of an Era Audio CD, *"Society Blues,"* 1921; *"Rhapsody in Blue"*; *"West End Blues"*; *"East St. Louis Toodle-oo,"* 1927; *"I, Too, Am America"*

INSTRUCT

Develop Understanding
Discuss with students the role of mass media and African American migration in the development of the Jazz Age.

Monitor Comprehension
Have students explain the difference between the writers who were called a Lost Generation and those who were part of the Harlem Renaissance.

Targeted Resources

❑ Learning Styles Lesson Plans booklet, p. 42 **L2**
❑ Skills for Life booklet, p. 22 **L1**
❑ Learning with Documents booklet, p. 59 **L3**
❑ Biography, Literature, and Comparing Primary Sources booklet, *The Weary Blues,* p. 67 **L3**
❑ Exploring Primary Sources in U.S. History CD-ROM, *As I Grew Older, Langston Hughes* **L3**

ASSESS/RETEACH

Monitor Progress
Assess students' completed graphic organizers using the Section Reading Support Transparency.

Assess
Use the Section 2 Quiz to evaluate student understanding of key concepts in this section.

Reteach
Assign students the Guide to the Essentials.

Homework _____
_____

Targeted Resources

❑ Section Reading Support Transparencies **L1** **ELL**
❑ Guided Reading and Review booklet, p. 84 **L1**
❑ Section 2 Quiz, Units 7/8 booklet, p. 5 **L1** **L2**
❑ Guide to the Essentials, p. 105 **L1** **L2**
❑ Social Studies Skills Tutor CD-ROM **L1**

Key
L1 Basic to Average   **L3** Average to Advanced
L2 For All Students   **ELL** English Language Learners

LESSON PLAN 20.3
Section 3 Cultural Conflicts

1 Period, .5 Block

Section Objectives

1. Learn about the effects of Prohibition on society.
2. Discover the issues of religion that were at the core of the Scopes trial.
3. Find out how racial tensions changed after World War I.

Vocabulary bootleggers • speakeasies • fundamentalism • Scopes trial

Local Standards

FOCUS

Teach Key Concepts and Vocabulary
Ask students to identify the major cultural conflicts that arose after World War I and explain the differences in values between people on each side of those conflicts.

Build Background Knowledge
Have students explain how Prohibition encouraged the rise of organized crime.

Targeted Resources
❑ Activating Prior Knowledge, TE p. 699 **L1**
❑ Sounds of an Era Audio CD, *Billy Sunday, 1923*

INSTRUCT

Develop Understanding
Discuss with students the divisions in American society, as revealed in the Scopes trial and in the racial tensions of the 1920s.

Monitor Comprehension
Ask students what issues—both legal and social—were at stake in the Scopes trial.

Targeted Resources
❑ Learning Styles Lesson Plans booklet, p. 43 **L2**
❑ Biography, Literature, and Comparing Primary Sources booklet, *On the Eighteenth Amendment*, p. 135 **L3**
❑ Presentation Pro CD-ROM, Chapter 20, Section 3 **L1**

ASSESS/RETEACH

Monitor Progress
Assess students' completed graphic organizers using the Section Reading Support Transparency. Review the answers to the Guided Reading and Review worksheet.

Assess
Use the Section 3 Quiz to evaluate student understanding of key concepts in this section.

Reteach
Assign students the section summary in the Guide to the Essentials.

Targeted Resources
❑ Section Reading Support Transparencies **L1** **ELL**
❑ Guided Reading and Review booklet, p. 85 **L1**
❑ Section 3 Quiz, Units 7/8 booklet, p. 6 **L1** **L2**
❑ Guide to the Essentials, p. 106 **L1** **L2**
❑ Guided Reading Audiotapes **ELL**
❑ Student Edition on Audio CD **ELL**
❑ Chapter Summary, Units 7/8 booklet, p. 3 **L1** **ELL**
❑ GoOnline: PHSchool.com, Chapter 20 Self-Test, Web Code: mra-7204
❑ Chapter 20 Tests, Units 7/8 booklet, pp. 7, 10

Homework _____

_____

Key
L1 Basic to Average   **L3** Average to Advanced
L2 For All Students   **ELL** English Language Learners

LESSON PLAN 21.1
A Republican Decade
1 Period, .5 Block

Section Objectives

1. Learn about events that fueled the Red Scare of the early 1920s.
2. Find out about conflicts that led to the major labor strikes of 1919.
3. See how Republican leadership during the Harding and Coolidge presidencies shaped the 1920s.
4. Discover the issues that shaped the presidential election of 1928.

Vocabulary communism • Red Scare • isolationism • disarmament • quota • Teapot Dome scandal • Kellogg-Briand Pact

Local Standards

FOCUS

Teach Key Concepts and Vocabulary
Ask students to identify the policies that Republican Presidents followed to encourage security and stability after the turmoil of World War I.

Build Background Knowledge
Remind students that Americans had distrusted "entangling alliances" since the time of George Washington, but that the nation's growth as a world power made isolation more and more difficult to maintain.

Targeted Resources

❏ Activating Prior Knowledge, TE p. 712 **L1**
❏ Sounds of an Era Audio CD, *Warren Harding; Calvin Coolidge*, 1924

INSTRUCT

Develop Understanding
Discuss the effects that the Russian Revolution had on American society.

Monitor Comprehension
Ask students how labor strikes sparked Americans' fears of communism, immigrants, and violence.

Targeted Resources

❏ Learning Styles Lesson Plans booklet, p. 44 **L2**
❏ Learning with Documents booklet, *Industrializing the USSR*, p. 26 **L3**
❏ Biography, Literature, and Comparing Primary Sources booklet, *Walter Lippmann*, p. 26 **L3**
❏ Prentice Hall U.S. History Video Collection, Vol. 17, *The Roaring Twenties*

ASSESS/RETEACH

Monitor Progress
Assess students' completed graphic organizers, using the Section Reading Support Transparency.

Assess
Use the Section 1 Quiz to evaluate student understanding of key concepts in this section.

Reteach
Assign students the Guide to the Essentials.

Targeted Resources

❏ Section Reading Support Transparencies **L1** **ELL**
❏ Guided Reading and Review booklet, p. 86 **L1**
❏ Section 1 Quiz, Units 7/8 booklet, p. 14 **L1** **L2**
❏ Guide to the Essentials, p. 108 **L1** **L2**
❏ Student Edition on Audio CD **ELL**

Homework _____

_____

Key
L1 Basic to Average   **L3** Average to Advanced
L2 For All Students   **ELL** English Language Learners

LESSON PLAN 21.2

A Business Boom

🕐 *1 Period, .5 Block*

Section Objectives

1. Understand the role businesses and consumers play in a consumer economy.
2. Find out how Henry Ford and the automobile were important to the 1920s.
3. Discover the ways in which industrial growth affected the economy of the 1920s.
4. See how the economic boom bypassed some people and benefited others.

Local Standards

Vocabulary consumer economy • installment plan • Gross National Product (GNP) • assembly line

---

FOCUS

Teach Key Concepts and Vocabulary
Ask students to identify and describe the economic development that led to a huge business expansion during the 1920s.

Build Background Knowledge
Explain that after World War I, isolation-minded Americans focused on improving their lives at home. Rising incomes and a new materialism resulted in an economy that depended on a high rate of consumer spending.

Targeted Resources

❏ Activating Prior Knowledge, TE p. 723 **L1**
❏ Color Transparencies, *The Way It Works*, H17 **L2**
❏ Sounds of an Era Audio CD, *Will Rogers*, 1925

INSTRUCT

Develop Understanding
Have students discuss how higher wages, buying on credit, advertising, and rising productivity were all linked and how they worked together to keep the economy booming.

Monitor Comprehension
Ask students to explain how increasing consumer demand encouraged Henry Ford to be innovative in the manufacture of automobiles.

Targeted Resources

❏ Learning Styles Lesson Plans booklet, p. 45 **L2**
❏ Learning with Documents booklet, *Advertising Techniques of the 1920s*, p. 60 **L3**
❏ Biography, Literature, and Comparing Primary Sources booklet, *Superpower*, pp. 68–69; *On the McNary-Haugen Bill (1927)*, pp. 137–138 **L3**

ASSESS/RETEACH

Monitor Progress
Assess students' completed graphic organizers using the Section Reading Support Transparency.

Assess
Use the Section 2 Quiz to evaluate student understanding of key concepts in this section.

Reteach
Assign students the Guide to the Essentials.

Targeted Resources

❏ Section Reading Support Transparencies **L1** **ELL**
❏ Guided Reading and Review booklet, p. 87 **L1**
❏ Section 2 Quiz, Units 7/8 booklet, p. 15 **L1** **L2**
❏ Guide to the Essentials, p. 109 **L1** **L2**
❏ Guided Reading Audiotapes **ELL**

Homework _____

_____

Key
L1 Basic to Average   **L3** Average to Advanced
L2 For All Students   **ELL** English Language Learners

Teacher_____ Class _____ Date_____ M T W T F

LESSON PLAN 21.3

The Economy in the Late 1920s

⏰ *.5 Period, .25 Block*

Section Objectives

1. See why the economy in the late 1920s appeared healthy to most Americans.
2. Observe the danger signs that were present in the economy of the late 1920s.

Vocabulary welfare capitalism • speculation • buying on margin

Local Standards

FOCUS	**Targeted Resources**

Teach Key Concepts and Vocabulary
Ask students to explain why most Americans felt optimistic about the economy.

Build Background Knowledge
Remind students that many Americans had prospered from the booming economy, which appeared to be stable and strong.

❏ Activating Prior Knowledge, TE p. 730 **L1**

INSTRUCT	**Targeted Resources**

Develop Understanding
Discuss the economic danger signs that were hidden behind the bright glow of the growing economy, including uneven prosperity, rising personal debt, high-risk stock-market investing, and overproduction.

Monitor Comprehension
Ask students how farmers and factory workers fared during this generally prosperous time.

❏ Presentation Pro CD-ROM, Chapter 21, Section 3 **L1**

ASSESS/RETEACH	**Targeted Resources**

Monitor Progress
Assess students' completed graphic organizers using the Section Reading Support Transparency. Review the answers to the Guided Reading and Review worksheet.

Assess
Use the Section 3 Quiz to evaluate student understanding of key concepts in this section.

Reteach
Assign students the section summary in the Guide to the Essentials.

❏ Section Reading Support Transparencies **L1** **ELL**
❏ Guided Reading and Review booklet, p. 88 **L1**
❏ Section 3 Quiz, Units 7/8 booklet, p. 16 **L1** **L2**
❏ Guide to the Essentials, p. 110 **L1** **L2**
❏ Guided Reading Audiotapes **ELL**
❏ Student Edition on Audio CD **ELL**
❏ Chapter Summary, Units 7/8 booklet, p. 13 **L1** **ELL**
❏ GoOnline: PHSchool.com, Chapter 21 Self-Test, Web Code: mra-7214
❏ Chapter 21 Tests, Units 7/8 booklet, pp. 17, 20

Homework _____

_____

Key
L1 Basic to Average **L3** Average to Advanced
L2 For All Students **ELL** English Language Learners

LESSON PLAN 22.1
The Stock Market Crash
⏱ *.5 Period, .25 Block*

Section Objectives

1. Learn about events that led to the stock market's Great Crash in 1929.
2. See how the Great Crash produced a ripple effect throughout the nation's economy.
3. Become familiar with the main causes of the Great Depression.

Local Standards

Vocabulary Dow Jones Industrial Average • Black Tuesday • Great Crash • business cycle • Great Depression

FOCUS

Teach Key Concepts and Vocabulary
Ask students to identify the events that led to the Great Crash of October 1929.

Build Background Knowledge
Explain that the stock market crash triggered the worst depression that Americans had ever experienced.

Targeted Resources

❏ Activating Prior Knowledge, TE p. 740 **L1**
❏ Color Transparencies, *American Photo*, F7 **L2**

INSTRUCT

Develop Understanding
Discuss the ripple effects of the crash, including its immediate impact on banks and businesses as well as its longer-term impact on workers and farmers.

Monitor Comprehension
Ask students to explain why the Great Crash affected not just the United States but countries around the world.

Targeted Resources

❏ Biography, Literature, and Comparing Primary Sources booklet, *The Stock Market Crash*, p. 70 **L3**
❏ Presentation Pro CD-ROM, Chapter 22, Section 1 **L1**
❏ Prentice Hall U.S. History Video Collection, Vol. 18, *The Great Depression and the New Deal*

ASSESS/RETEACH

Monitor Progress
Assess students' completed graphic organizers using the Section Reading Support Transparency. Review the answers to the Guided Reading and Review worksheet.

Assess
Use the Section 1 Quiz to evaluate student understanding of key concepts in this section.

Reteach
Assign students the section summary in the Guide to the Essentials.

Targeted Resources

❏ Section Reading Support Transparencies **L1** **ELL**
❏ Guided Reading and Review booklet, p. 89 **L1**
❏ Section 1 Quiz, Units 7/8 booklet, p. 24 **L1** **L2**
❏ Guide to the Essentials, p. 112 **L1** **L2**
❏ Guided Reading Audiotapes **ELL**
❏ Student Edition on Audio CD **ELL**

Homework _____

_____

Key
L1 Basic to Average
L2 For All Students
L3 Average to Advanced
ELL English Language Learners

LESSON PLAN 22.2
Social Effects of the Depression
🕐 *1 Period, .5 Block*

Section Objectives
1. Understand how poverty spread during the Great Depression.
2. Find out about social problems that were caused by poverty in the 1930s.
3. Discover how some people struggled to survive hard times.

Vocabulary Hooverville • Dust Bowl

Local Standards

FOCUS

Teach Key Concepts and Vocabulary
Ask students to discuss how the Great Depression changed Americans' lives.

Build Background Knowledge
Explain that at first many Americans thought the economy would bounce back, but as the Depression dragged on more and more people lost their jobs, their homes, and their optimism.

Targeted Resources
❏ Activating Prior Knowledge, TE p. 745 **L1**
❏ Color Transparencies, Historical Maps, A35 **L2**
❏ Sounds of an Era Audio CD, *"The Grapes of Wrath"*

INSTRUCT

Develop Understanding
Ask students to identify who was most severely affected by the Depression. Discuss how the Depression affected men, women, farm families, and minority Americans.

Monitor Comprehension
Ask students to describe how the Depression affected people's physical and psychological health.

Targeted Resources
❏ Learning Styles Lesson Plans booklet, p. 46 **L2**
❏ Skills for Life booklet, p. 24 **L1**
❏ Presentation Pro CD-ROM, Chapter 22, Section 2 **L1**
❏ Exploring Primary Sources in U.S. History CD-ROM, *The Grapes of Wrath*, John Steinbeck; *Depression Photograph*, Dorothea Lange **L3**

ASSESS/RETEACH

Monitor Progress
Assess students' completed graphic organizers using the Section Reading Support Transparency. Review the answers to the Guided Reading and Review worksheet.

Assess
Use the Section 2 Quiz to evaluate student understanding of key concepts in this section.

Reteach
Assign students the section summary in the Guide to the Essentials.

Targeted Resources
❏ Section Reading Support Transparencies **L1** **ELL**
❏ Guided Reading and Review booklet, p. 90 **L1**
❏ Section 2 Quiz, Units 7/8 booklet, p. 25 **L1** **L2**
❏ Guide to the Essentials, p. 113 **L1** **L2**
❏ Social Studies Skills Tutor CD-ROM **L1**
❏ Guided Reading Audiotapes **ELL**
❏ Student Edition on Audio CD **ELL**

Homework _____

_____

Key
L1 Basic to Average **L3** Average to Advanced
L2 For All Students **ELL** English Language Learners

LESSON PLAN 22.3
Surviving the Great Depression
🕐 .5 Period, .25 Block

Section Objectives

1. Read about ways Americans pulled together to survive the Great Depression.
2. See the signs of change Americans began to notice in the early 1930s.

Vocabulary penny auction • Twenty-first Amendment

Local Standards

FOCUS

Teach Key Concepts and Vocabulary
Ask students to describe the characteristics that helped Americans survive the hard times of the Great Depression.

Build Background Knowledge
Explain to students that Americans never forgot the painful economic lessons they learned during the Great Depression, but that many of them also carried with them fond memories of how people pulled together to help one another through this rough period.

Targeted Resources

❏ Activating Prior Knowledge, TE p. 752 **L1**

INSTRUCT

Develop Understanding
Discuss how the Depression brought out the best in many Americans, who showed kindness and charity toward others and used humor to help them endure the many hardships.

Monitor Comprehension
Ask students to explain how the construction of the Empire State Building affected Americans.

Targeted Resources

❏ Biography, Literature, and Comparing Primary Sources booklet, *Babe Didrickson Zaharias*, p. 27 **L3**

❏ Presentation Pro CD-ROM, Chapter 22, Section 3 **L1**

❏ Exploring Primary Sources in U.S. History CD-ROM, *This Land Is Your Land, Woody Guthrie* **L3**

❏ American Heritage, My Brush With History, *Afternoon in the Ballpark,* Student Edition pp. 764–765, Videotape

---

ASSESS/RETEACH

Monitor Progress
Assess students' completed graphic organizers using the Section Reading Support Transparency.

Assess
Use the Section 3 Quiz to evaluate student understanding of key concepts in this section.

Reteach
Assign students the Guide to the Essentials.

Targeted Resources

❏ Section Reading Support Transparencies **L1** **ELL**

❏ Guided Reading and Review booklet, p. 91 **L1**

❏ Section 3 Quiz, Units 7/8 booklet, p. 26 **L1** **L2**

❏ Guide to the Essentials, p. 114 **L1** **L2**

❏ Guided Reading Audiotapes **ELL**

❏ Student Edition on Audio CD **ELL**

Homework _____

_____

Key
L1 Basic to Average   **L3** Average to Advanced
L2 For All Students   **ELL** English Language Learners

LESSON PLAN 22.4

The Election of 1932

🕐 *1 Period, .5 Block*

Section Objectives

1. Find out how President Hoover responded to the Great Depression.
2. Learn what Roosevelt meant when he offered Americans a "new deal."
3. Realize why the election of 1932 was a significant turning point in American politics.

Local Standards

Vocabulary Hawley-Smoot tariff • Reconstruction Finance Corporation (RFC) • Bonus Army

---

FOCUS

Teach Key Concepts and Vocabulary
Ask students to describe how the newly elected President, Franklin Roosevelt, changed the federal government's strategy for dealing with the Depression.

Build Background Knowledge
Explain that President Hoover, a successful businessman, believed in self-reliance. He thought voluntary actions by businesses—such as keeping wage rates up—were the best way to end the nation's economic crisis.

Targeted Resources

❏ Activating Prior Knowledge, TE p. 756 **L1**
❏ Color Transparencies, *Political Cartoons*, B12 **L2**
❏ Sounds of an Era Audio CD, *Breakup of the Bonus Army*, 1932

INSTRUCT

Develop Understanding
Ask students what programs Roosevelt had in mind when he promised the American people a "new deal." Discuss why Roosevelt's approach appealed to voters.

Monitor Comprehension
Ask students to discuss Roosevelt's qualifications to lead the nation during the Depression.

Targeted Resources

❏ Learning Styles Lesson Plans booklet, p. 47 **L2**
❏ Learning with Documents booklet, Franklin D. Roosevelt, *First Inaugural Address*, p. 87 **L3**
❏ Biography, Literature, and Comparing Primary Sources booklet, *On Ending the Depression*, p. 139 **L3**
❏ Presentation Pro CD-ROM, Chapter 22, Section 4 **L1**

ASSESS/RETEACH

Monitor Progress
Assess students' completed graphic organizers using the Section Reading Support Transparency.

Assess
Use the Section 4 Quiz to evaluate student understanding of key concepts in this section.

Reteach
Assign students the section summary in the Guide to the Essentials.

Targeted Resources

❏ Section Reading Support Transparencies **L1** **ELL**
❏ Guided Reading and Review booklet, p. 92 **L1**
❏ Section 4 Quiz, Units 7/8 booklet, p. 27 **L1** **L2**
❏ Guide to the Essentials, p. 115 **L1** **L2**
❏ GoOnline: PHSchool.com, Chapter 22 Self-Test, Web Code: mra-7225
❏ Chapter 22 Tests, Units 7/8 booklet, pp. 28, 31

Homework _____

_____

Key
L1 Basic to Average   **L3** Average to Advanced
L2 For All Students   **ELL** English Language Learners

LESSON PLAN 23.1
Forging a New Deal
🕐 *1 Period, .5 Block*

Section Objectives	**Local Standards**

Section Objectives

1. Explore Franklin and Eleanor Roosevelt's roles in restoring the nation's hope.
2. Learn about the major New Deal programs created in the first hundred days, and about FDR's key players in these programs.
3. Discover what caused the New Deal to falter.
4. Review the key goals and accomplishments of the second New Deal.
5. Interpret the significance of the outcome of the 1936 election.

Vocabulary New Deal • hundred days • public works program • Civilian Conservation Corps (CCC) • Agricultural Adjustment Administration (AAA) • Tennessee Valley Authority (TVA) • Second New Deal • Wagner Act • closed shop • Social Security system

FOCUS

Teach Key Concepts and Vocabulary
Ask students to explain FDR's actions during the hundred days aimed to restore the nation's hope, and discuss how successful those actions were.

Build Background Knowledge
Explain that Roosevelt had promised to take "action now." However, the new programs failed to improve the economy significantly, leaving the door open for a Second New Deal.

Targeted Resources
❏ Activating Prior Knowledge, TE p. 768 **L1**
❏ Color Transparencies, *Cause-and-Effect Charts*, D9 **L2**
❏ Historical Outline Map Book, *Tennessee Valley Authority*, p. 63 **L1**
❏ Sounds of an Era Audio CD, *President Roosevelt's First Inauguration Speech*, 1933; *President Roosevelt's First "Fireside Chat,"* 1933; *Dorothy Thompson on Eleanor Roosevelt*, 1936

INSTRUCT

Develop Understanding
Ask students to name and describe the programs FDR created, and discuss how the Second New Deal attempted to remedy the earlier problems.

Monitor Comprehension
Ask students how FDR's choice of advisors and policymakers reflected his commitment to change.

Targeted Resources
❏ Learning with Documents booklet, *A Fireside Chat; The NIRA*, p. 28; *Promoting the WPA*, p. 62 **L3**
❏ Exploring Primary Sources in U.S. History CD-ROM, First Inaugural Address, Franklin D. Roosevelt **L3**

ASSESS/RETEACH

Monitor Progress
Assess students' completed graphic organizers using the Section Reading Support Transparency.

Assess
Use the Section 1 Quiz to evaluate student understanding of key concepts in this section.

Reteach
Assign students the Guide to the Essentials.

Targeted Resources
❏ Section Reading Support Transparencies **L1 ELL**
❏ Guided Reading and Review booklet, p. 93 **L1**
❏ Section 1 Quiz, Units 7/8 booklet, p. 35 **L1 L2**
❏ Guide to the Essentials, p. 117 **L1 L2**

Homework _____
_____

Key
L1 Basic to Average   **L3** Average to Advanced
L2 For All Students   **ELL** English Language Learners

LESSON PLAN 23.2

The New Deal's Critics

🕐 *1 Period, .5 Block*

Section Objectives

1. Learn about some of the New Deal's shortcomings and limitations.
2. Discover the chief complaints of FDR's critics inside and outside of politics.
3. See how the court-packing fiasco harmed FDR's reputation.

Vocabulary American Liberty League • demagogue • nationalization • deficit spending

Local Standards

FOCUS

Teach Key Concepts and Vocabulary

Ask students to explain why many people were sharply critical of the New Deal. Have them discuss the split between those who thought it did too much and those who thought it did not do enough.

Build Background Knowledge

Explain that Americans had high expectations that the New Deal would end the Depression, and many people were disappointed when it failed.

Targeted Resources

❏ Activating Prior Knowledge, TE p. 777 **L1**
❏ Color Transparencies, *Political Cartoons*, B13 **L2**
❏ Sounds of an Era Audio CD, Marian Anderson; *"Share the Wealth,"* Huey Long

---

INSTRUCT

Develop Understanding

Discuss how the New Deal failed to address the problems of many women and African Americans, and have students summarize the complaints of other critics, including Father Coughlin and Huey Long.

Monitor Comprehension

Ask students why FDR's attempt to "pack" the Supreme Court was a bad idea.

Targeted Resources

❏ Learning Styles Lesson Plans booklet, p. 49 **L2**
❏ Skills for Life booklet, p. 25 **L1**
❏ Biography, Literature, and Comparing Primary Sources booklet, *In Search of Work: African Americans*, p. 71 **L3**
❏ Presentation Pro CD-ROM, Chapter 23, Section 2 **L1**

ASSESS/RETEACH

Monitor Progress

Assess students' completed graphic organizers using the Section Reading Support Transparency. Review the answers to the Guided Reading and Review worksheet.

Assess

Use the Section 2 Quiz to evaluate student understanding of key concepts in this section.

Reteach

Assign students the Guide to the Essentials.

Targeted Resources

❏ Section Reading Support Transparencies **L1** **ELL**
❏ Guided Reading and Review booklet, p. 94 **L1**
❏ Section 2 Quiz, Units 7/8 booklet, p. 36 **L1** **L2**
❏ Guide to the Essentials, p. 118 **L1** **L2**
❏ Social Studies Skills Tutor CD-ROM **L1**
❏ Guided Reading Audiotapes **ELL**
❏ Student Edition on Audio CD **ELL**

Homework _____

_____

Key
L1 Basic to Average   **L3** Average to Advanced
L2 For All Students   **ELL** English Language Learners

LESSON PLAN 23.3
Last Days of the New Deal
⏱ *1 Period, .5 Block*

Section Objectives

1. Learn about factors that led to the recession of 1937 and about the Roosevelt administration's response to this situation.
2. Find out about triumphs and setbacks experienced by unions during the New Deal era.
3. Discover some effects of the New Deal on American culture.
4. See what lasting effects can be attributed to the New Deal.

Local Standards

Vocabulary recession • national debt • revenue • coalition • sit-down strike

---

FOCUS

Teach Key Concepts and Vocabulary
Ask students to describe the effects of the New Deal on the nation's political, social, and cultural life and to describe ways that the New Deal's impact is still felt today.

Build Background Knowledge
Explain that although the New Deal did not end the Depression, its policies and programs substantially changed American society.

Targeted Resources
❏ Activating Prior Knowledge, TE p. 785 **L1**
❏ Sounds of an Era Audio CD, *"King Porter Stomp,"* Benny Goodman; *"The People, Yes,"* Carl Sandburg

---

INSTRUCT

Develop Understanding
Discuss the changes that the New Deal brought about, including those affecting labor unions and the arts.

Monitor Comprehension
Ask students what the recession of 1937 revealed about the New Deal and the economy.

Targeted Resources
❏ Biography, Literature, and Comparing Primary Sources booklet, *Emma Tenayuca*, p. 28 **L3**
❏ Presentation Pro CD-ROM, Chapter 23, Section 3 **L1**

ASSESS/RETEACH

Monitor Progress
Assess students' completed graphic organizers using the Section Reading Support Transparency. Review the answers to the Guided Reading and Review worksheet.

Assess
Use the Section 3 Quiz to evaluate student understanding of key concepts in this section.

Reteach
Assign students the Guide to the Essentials.

Targeted Resources
❏ Section Reading Support Transparency **L1** **ELL**
❏ Guided Reading and Review booklet, p. 95 **L1**
❏ Section 3 Quiz, Units 7/8 booklet, p. 37 **L1** **L2**
❏ Guide to the Essentials, p. 119 **L1** **L2**
❏ Chapter Summary, Units 7/8 booklet, p. 34 **L1** **ELL**
❏ GoOnline: PHSchool.com, Chapter 23 Self-Test, Web Code: mra-7234
❏ Chapter 23 Tests, Units 7/8 booklet, pp. 38, 41

Homework _____

_____

Key
L1 Basic to Average **L3** Average to Advanced
L2 For All Students **ELL** English Language Learners

LESSON PLAN 24.1

The Rise of Dictators

1 Period, .5 Block

Section Objectives

1. Find out how the government and the economy of the Soviet Union changed under Stalin.
2. Discover the origins and goals of Italy's fascist government.
3. See how Hitler rose to power in Germany and Europe in the 1930s.
4. Learn about the causes and results of the Spanish Civil War.

Vocabulary Powers • appeasement

Local Standards

FOCUS

Teach Key Concepts and Vocabulary
Ask students to explain how dictators were able to rise to power in the Soviet Union, Italy, and Germany after World War I, despite widespread resistance.

Build Background Knowledge
Explain that World War I, and later the Great Depression, ruined the Soviet Union, Italy, and Germany economically. Dictators promised to return their nations to prosperity.

Targeted Resources
❏ Activating Prior Knowledge, TE p. 800 **L1**
❏ Color Transparencies, Historical Maps, A36, A37 **L2**
❏ Historical Outline Map Book, *Aggression in Europe*, p. 64 **L1**

INSTRUCT

Develop Understanding
Discuss the dictators' economic plans, and ask students how the dictators used territorial expansion as a way to bolster national pride.

Monitor Comprehension
Ask students to explain how a political struggle in Spain mirrored what was going on in Germany and Italy.

Targeted Resources
❏ Learning Styles Lesson Plans booklet, p. 50 **L2**
❏ Biography, Literature, and Comparing Primary Sources booklet, *Winston Churchill*, p. 29 **L3**
❏ Exploring Primary Sources in U.S. History CD-ROM, *Berlin Diary*, William Shirer **L3**
❏ Prentice Hall U.S. History Video Collection, Vol. 19, World War II

ASSESS/RETEACH

Monitor Progress
Assess students' completed graphic organizers using the Section Reading Support Transparency.

Assess
Use the Section 1 Quiz to evaluate student understanding of key concepts in this section.

Reteach
Assign students the Guide to the Essentials.

Targeted Resources
❏ Section Reading Support Transparencies **L1** **ELL**
❏ Guided Reading and Review booklet, p. 96 **L1**
❏ Section 1 Quiz, Units 7/8 booklet, p. 49 **L1** **L2**
❏ Guide to the Essentials, p. 121 **L1** **L2**
❏ Guided Reading Audiotapes **ELL**
❏ Student Edition on Audio CD **ELL**

Homework _____

_____

Key
L1 Basic to Average   **L3** Average to Advanced
L2 For All Students   **ELL** English Language Learners

LESSON PLAN 24.2

Europe Goes to War

🕐 *.5 Period, .25 Block*

Section Objectives

Local Standards

1. Understand how the German invasion of Poland led to war with Britain and France.
2. See what wartime victories and setbacks Germany experienced in western Europe.
3. Find out why the Battle of Britain was an important victory for Britain.

Vocabulary *blitzkrieg* • collaboration • Resistance • Allies

FOCUS

Teach Key Concepts and Vocabulary
Ask students to identify the advantages Britain had over Germany as the two countries fought the Battle of Britain.

Build Background Knowledge
Remind students that the tactic of blitzkrieg had successfully propelled the German army as far as the English Channel.

Targeted Resources
❏ Activating Prior Knowledge, TE p. 807 **L1**
❏ Color Transparencies, Historical Maps, A38 **L2**
❏ Historical Outline Map Book, *World War II in Europe and North Africa*, p. 65 **L1**
❏ Sounds of an Era Audio CD, Winston Churchill, 1940; *Edward R. Murrow on the London Blitz*, 1940

INSTRUCT

Develop Understanding
Discuss with students how Hitler combined military and political strategies to ease the fears of his main opponents, invade neighboring countries, and eliminate the danger of a Soviet invasion.

Monitor Comprehension
Ask students to judge the effectiveness of Chamberlain's policy of appeasement.

Targeted Resources
❏ Learning Styles Lesson Plans booklet, p. 51 **L2**
❏ Skills for Life booklet, p. 26 **L1**
❏ Learning with Documents booklet, *Germans March at the Arc de Triomphe*, p. 63 **L3**
❏ Biography, Literature, and Comparing Primary Sources booklet, *On Arming Europe*, p. 143; *This Was His Hour*, p. 72 **L3**
❏ Presentation Pro CD-ROM, Chapter 24, Section 2 **L1**

ASSESS/RETEACH

Monitor Progress
Assess students' completed graphic organizers using the Section Reading Support Transparency.

Assess
Use the Section 2 Quiz to evaluate student understanding of key concepts in this section.

Reteach
Assign students the section summary in the Guide to the Essentials.

Targeted Resources
❏ Section Reading Support Transparencies **L1 ELL**
❏ Guided Reading and Review booklet, p. 97 **L1**
❏ Section 2 Quiz, Units 7/8 booklet, p. 50 **L1 L2**
❏ Guide to the Essentials, p. 122 **L1 L2**
❏ Social Studies Skills Tutor CD-ROM **L1**
❏ Guided Reading Audiotapes **ELL**
❏ Student Edition on Audio CD **ELL**

Homework _____

_____

Key
L1 Basic to Average
L2 For All Students
L3 Average to Advanced
ELL English Language Learners

LESSON PLAN 24.3
Japan Builds an Empire
🕐 .5 Period, .25 Block

Section Objectives

1. Discover the causes and effects of Japan's growing military power.
2. See why the Manchurian Incident was a turning point for Japan's civil government.
3. Find out about the initial outcome of Japan's war against China.
4. Learn why Japan looked beyond China for future expansion.

Vocabulary Manchurian Incident • puppet state • Burma Road • Greater East Asia Co-Prosperity Sphere

Local Standards

FOCUS

Teach Key Concepts and Vocabulary
Ask students to describe how Japan reacted when the United States and other nations condemned its expansion into Manchuria and the rest of China.

Build Background Knowledge
Remind students that Japan had a long history of isolationism, and that in the 1930s its military increasingly influenced government policy.

Targeted Resources
❏ Activating Prior Knowledge, TE p. 813 **L1**
❏ Color Transparencies, Historical Maps, A39 **L2**
❏ Historical Outline Map Book, *World War II in the Pacific*, p. 66 **L1**

INSTRUCT

Develop Understanding
Discuss how Japan pressed for control of China and how the United States, limited by a series of Neutrality Acts, could only call for a "quarantine" of Japan. Ask for opinions about what might have happened if the United States had not had an official policy of neutrality.

Monitor Comprehension
Ask students to explain why the Manchurian Incident was a turning point in the Japanese military's domination of the civilian government.

Targeted Resources
❏ Presentation Pro CD-ROM, Chapter 24, Section 3 **L1**

ASSESS/RETEACH

Monitor Progress
Assess students' completed graphic organizers using the Section Reading Support Transparency.

Assess
Use the Section 3 Quiz to evaluate student understanding of key concepts in this section.

Reteach
Assign students the Guide to the Essentials.

Homework _____
_____

Targeted Resources
❏ Section Reading Support Transparencies **L1 ELL**
❏ Guided Reading and Review booklet, p. 98 **L1 ELL**
❏ Section 3 Quiz, Units 7/8 booklet, p. 51 **L1 L2**
❏ Guide to the Essentials, p. 123 **L1 L2**
❏ Guided Reading Audiotapes **ELL**

Key
L1 Basic to Average   **L3** Average to Advanced
L2 For All Students   **ELL** English Language Learners

LESSON PLAN 24.4
From Isolationism to War
⏰ *.5 Period, .25 Block*

Section Objectives

1. Find out why the United States chose neutrality in the 1930s.
2. See how American involvement in the European conflict grew from 1939 to 1941.
3. Discover why Japan's attack on Pearl Harbor led the United States to declare war.

Local Standards

Vocabulary Neutrality Acts • cash and carry • America First Committee • Lend-Lease Act

FOCUS	**Targeted Resources**

Teach Key Concepts and Vocabulary
Ask students to describe how the United States responded in the 1930s to the growing world-wide conflict.

Build Background Knowledge
Remind students that the United States was well aware that the aggressive actions of Germany, Italy, and Japan threatened world peace.

❏ Activating Prior Knowledge, TE p. 817 **L1**
❏ Color Transparencies, Historical Maps, A40 **L2**
❏ Sounds of an Era Audio CD, *Broadcast from KGU, Honolulu, December 7, 1941; Broadcast from Washington, December 7, 1941; Roosevelt's Declaration of War, 1941; "We Hold These Truths,"* December 15, 1941

INSTRUCT	**Targeted Resources**

Develop Understanding
Discuss American reluctance to enter the war and how FDR managed to push for greater support of Britain.

Monitor Comprehension
Ask students to identify the events that overcame American reluctance to enter the war.

❏ Learning with Documents booklet, *Einstein's Letter to FDR,* p. 29; Franklin D. Roosevelt, *Message Asking for War Against Japan,* p. 88 **L3**
❏ Presentation Pro CD-ROM, Chapter 24, Section 4 **L1**
❏ Exploring Primary Sources in U.S. History CD-ROM, *Lend Lease; Pearl Harbor,* Daniel K. Inouye **L3**

ASSESS/RETEACH	**Targeted Resources**

Monitor Progress
Assess students' completed graphic organizers using the Section Reading Support Transparency. Review the answers to the Guided Reading and Review worksheet.

Assess
Use the Section 4 Quiz to evaluate student understanding of key concepts in this section.

Reteach
Assign students the section summary in the Guide to the Essentials.

❏ Section Reading Support Transparencies **L1** **ELL**
❏ Guided Reading and Review booklet, p. 99 **L1**
❏ Section 4 Quiz, Units 7/8 booklet, p. 52 **L1 L2**
❏ Guide to the Essentials, p. 124 **L1 L2**
❏ Guided Reading Audiotapes **ELL**
❏ Student Edition on Audio CD **ELL**
❏ Chapter Summary, Units 7/8 booklet, p. 48 **L1 ELL**
❏ GoOnline: PHSchool.com, Chapter 24 Self-Test, Web Code: mra-8245
❏ Chapter 24 Tests, Units 7/8 booklet, pp. 53, 56

Homework _____
_____

Key
L1 Basic to Average   **L3** Average to Advanced
L2 For All Students   **ELL** English Language Learners

LESSON PLAN 25.1
Mobilization
⏱ *1 Period, .5 Block*

| **Section Objectives** | **Local Standards** |

Section Objectives

1. Find out how Roosevelt mobilized the armed forces.
2. Learn about ways in which the government prepared the economy for war.
3. See how the war affected daily life on the home front.

Vocabulary Selective Training and Service Act • GI • Office of War Mobilization • Liberty ship • victory garden

FOCUS

Teach Key Concepts and Vocabulary
Ask students to explain how the shift into wartime production affected workers and businesses and changed daily life.

Build Background Knowledge
Explain that the goal of winning the war drove not only the government's foreign policy but also its domestic policy.

Targeted Resources
❏ Activating Prior Knowledge, TE p. 826 **L1**
❏ Color Transparencies, *Time Lines*, C7; *American Photo*, F8; *Fine Art*, E18 **L2**

INSTRUCT

Develop Understanding
Discuss the United States as the "arsenal of democracy" by asking students why it was crucial for American industries to make war supplies at the expense of consumer goods.

Monitor Comprehension
Ask students what action Congress took, before any declaration of war, to strengthen the armed forces.

Targeted Resources
❏ Learning Styles Lesson Plans booklet, p. 52 **L2**
❏ Presentation Pro CD-ROM, Chapter 25, Section 1 **L1**
❏ Exploring Primary Sources in U.S. History CD-ROM, *What Should You Bring Overseas?* Bill Steele **L3**
❏ Prentice Hall U.S. History Video Collection, Vol. 19, World War II

ASSESS/RETEACH

Monitor Progress
Assess students' completed graphic organizers using the Section Reading Support Transparency. Review the answers to the Guided Reading and Review worksheet.

Assess
Use the Section 1 Quiz to evaluate student understanding of key concepts in this section.

Reteach
Assign students the section summary in the Guide to the Essentials.

Targeted Resources
❏ Section Reading Support Transparencies **L1** **ELL**
❏ Guided Reading and Review booklet, p. 100 **L1**
❏ Section 1 Quiz, Units 7/8 booklet, p. 60 **L1** **L2**
❏ Guide to the Essentials, p. 126 **L1** **L2**
❏ Guided Reading Audiotapes **ELL**
❏ Student Edition on Audio CD **ELL**

Homework _____

_____

Key
L1 Basic to Average
L2 For All Students
L3 Average to Advanced
ELL English Language Learners

LESSON PLAN 25.2

Retaking Europe

1 Period, .5 Block

Section Objectives

1. See where Americans joined the struggle against the Axis.
2. Find out how the war in the Soviet Union changed from 1941 to 1943.
3. Learn about the role air power played in the war in Europe.
4. Read about why the invasion of Western Europe succeeded.
5. Discover some events that marked the end of the war in Europe.

Local Standards

Vocabulary Atlantic Charter • carpet bombing • D-Day • Battle of the Bulge

FOCUS

Teach Key Concepts and Vocabulary
Ask students whether Britain could have retaken Europe without American help.

Build Background Knowledge
Remind students that Britain was fighting the Axis Powers in North Africa but was otherwise on the defensive when the United States entered the war and that German U-boats threatened to shut down its vital Atlantic trade routes.

Targeted Resources

❏ Activating Prior Knowledge, TE p. 832 **L1**
❏ Color Transparencies, *The Way It Works*, H18; Historical Maps, A41, A42 **L2**
❏ Historical Outline Map Book, *World War II in Europe and North Africa*, p. 65; *Germany Divided*, p. 67 **L1**
❏ Sounds of an Era Audio CD, *D-Day Invasion*, 1944

INSTRUCT

Develop Understanding
Discuss the routes that the Allied armies followed in their drive to retake Europe.

Monitor Comprehension
Have students explain the significance of the Battle of Stalingrad, D-Day, and the Battle of the Bulge.

Targeted Resources

❏ Presentation Pro CD-ROM, Chapter 25, Section 2 **L1**
❏ Exploring Primary Sources in U.S. History CD-ROM, *"Gee, Mom, I Want to Go Home,"* army song **L3**

ASSESS/RETEACH

Monitor Progress
Assess students' completed graphic organizers using the Section Reading Support Transparency. Review the answers to the Guided Reading and Review worksheet.

Assess
Use the Section 2 Quiz to evaluate student understanding of key concepts in this section.

Reteach
Assign students the Guide to the Essentials.

Targeted Resources

❏ Section Reading Support Transparencies **L1** **ELL**
❏ Guided Reading and Review booklet, p. 101 **L1**
❏ Section 2 Quiz, Units 7/8 booklet, p. 61 **L1** **L2**
❏ Guide to the Essentials, p. 127 **L1** **L2**
❏ Guided Reading Audiotapes **ELL**
❏ Student Edition on Audio CD **ELL**

Homework _____
_____

Key
L1 Basic to Average
L2 For All Students
L3 Average to Advanced
ELL English Language Learners

LESSON PLAN 25.3
The Holocaust
🕐 *.5 Period, .25 Block*

Section Objectives

1. Find out about some ways in which Germany persecuted Jews in the 1930s.
2. See how Germany's policies toward Jews developed from murder into genocide.

Vocabulary anti-Semitism • Holocaust • concentration camp • Kristallnacht • Warsaw Ghetto • Wannsee Conference • death camp • War Refugee Board • Nuremberg Trials

Local Standards

FOCUS

Teach Key Concepts and Vocabulary
Ask students to describe how the Nazis went about killing some 6 million Jews and 5 to 6 million other Europeans.

Build Background Knowledge
Remind students that Jews had faced persecution for centuries, but the Holocaust went beyond persecution and beyond murder to genocide.

Targeted Resources
- ❏ Activating Prior Knowledge, TE p. 841 **L1**
- ❏ Color Transparencies, Historical Maps, A43 **L2**
- ❏ Sounds of an Era Audio CD, *Edward R. Murrow*

INSTRUCT

Develop Understanding
Ask students how Nazi policies developed during the 1930s to the point where they supported genocide. Have them make a time chart of these policies.

Monitor Comprehension
Ask students to describe the forms that Jewish resistance took.

Targeted Resources
- ❏ Presentation Pro CD-ROM, Chapter 25, Section 3 **L1**
- ❏ Exploring Primary Sources in U.S. History CD-ROM, *Night*, Elie Wiesel **L3**

ASSESS/RETEACH

Monitor Progress
Assess students' completed graphic organizers using the Section Reading Support Transparency. Review the answers to the Guided Reading and Review worksheet.

Assess
Use the Section 3 Quiz to evaluate student understanding of key concepts in this section.

Reteach
Assign students the section summary in the Guide to the Essentials.

Targeted Resources
- ❏ Section Reading Support Transparencies **L1** **ELL**
- ❏ Guided Reading and Review booklet, p. 102 **L1**
- ❏ Section 3 Quiz, Units 7/8 booklet, p. 62 **L1** **L2**
- ❏ Guide to the Essentials, p. 128 **L1** **L2**
- ❏ Guided Reading Audiotapes **ELL**
- ❏ Student Edition on Audio CD **ELL**

Homework _____
_____

Key
L1 Basic to Average   **L3** Average to Advanced
L2 For All Students   **ELL** English Language Learners

LESSON PLAN 25.4

The War in the Pacific

1 Period, .5 Block

Section Objectives

1. Learn about advances Japan made in Asia and the Pacific in late 1941 and 1942.
2. See which Allied victories turned the tide of war in the Pacific.
3. Read about the United States strategy in the struggle to reconquer the Pacific Islands.
4. Discover why the battles of Iwo Jima and Okinawa were important.
5. Understand how the Manhattan Project brought the war to an end.

Local Standards

Vocabulary Bataan Death March • Geneva Convention • Battle of the Coral Sea • Battle of Midway • Battle of Guadalcanal • island-hopping • Battle of Leyte Gulf • kamikaze • Battle of Iwo Jima • Battle of Okinawa • Manhattan Project

FOCUS

Teach Key Concepts and Vocabulary
Ask students to describe the war in the Pacific—how it started as a defensive struggle, turned into a bloody offensive campaign to retake Pacific islands, and ended with dropping nuclear bombs.

Build Background Knowledge
Remind students that the Allies' strategy was to concentrate on Europe before the Pacific.

Targeted Resources

❏ Activating Prior Knowledge, TE p. 846 **L1**
❏ Color Transparencies, Historical Maps, A44 **L2**
❏ Historical Outline Map Book, *World War II in the Pacific,* p. 66 **L1**
❏ Sounds of an Era Audio CD, *Roosevelt's Funeral,* April 1945; *President Truman,* 1945

INSTRUCT

Develop Understanding
Discuss Japan's successes between 1941 and 1942 and the winning, island-hopping strategy employed by the Allies from 1943 to 1945.

Monitor Comprehension
Ask students why the Battle of Okinawa was a significant strategic victory for the Allies.

Targeted Resources

❏ Learning with Documents booklet, *Guadalcanal,* p. 30 **L3**
❏ Biography, Literature, and Comparing Primary Sources booklet, *Hiroshima,* p. 74 **L3**
❏ Exploring Primary Sources in U.S. History CD-ROM, *Japanese Internment Photograph* **L3**
❏ American Heritage, My Brush With History, *Locking Horns With the Bull,* Student Edition pp. 864–865, Videotape

ASSESS/RETEACH

Monitor Progress
Assess students' completed graphic organizers using the Section Reading Support Transparency.

Assess
Use the Section 4 Quiz to evaluate student understanding of key concepts in this section.

Reteach
Assign students the Guide to the Essentials.

Homework _____
_____

Targeted Resources

❏ Section Reading Support Transparency **L1 ELL**
❏ Guided Reading and Review booklet, p. 103 **L1**
❏ Section 4 Quiz, Units 7/8 booklet, p. 63 **L1 L2**
❏ Guide to the Essentials, p. 129 **L1 L2**

Key
L1 Basic to Average   **L3** Average to Advanced
L2 For All Students   **ELL** English Language Learners

LESSON PLAN 25.5
The Social Impact of the War
⏱ *1 Period, .5 Block*

Section Objectives

1. Learn how African Americans, Mexican Americans, and Native Americans experienced the war at home.
2. Find out about difficulties Japanese Americans faced.
3. See how the war changed conditions for working women.

Local Standards

Vocabulary Congress of Racial Equality (CORE) • bracero • barrio • interned • Nisei

FOCUS	Targeted Resources
Teach Key Concepts and Vocabulary Ask students to describe the impact of the war on women and Americans of different ethnic groups. **Build Background Knowledge** Explain that the war opened doors for women and members of ethnic groups, but along with new opportunities came problems, mainly involving discrimination.	❏ Activating Prior Knowledge, TE p. 855 **L1** ❏ Sounds of an Era Audio CD, *Mary Anderson Director of the Women's Bureau*, 1942; "Rosie the Riveter"

INSTRUCT	Targeted Resources
Develop Understanding Discuss the job opportunities and related problems facing African Americans, Mexican Americans (and Mexicans), Native Americans, and women during the war. **Monitor Comprehension** Ask students to describe how Japanese Americans fared during the war.	❏ Learning Styles Lesson Plans booklet, p. 53 **L2** ❏ Learning with Documents booklet, *Campaigns on the Home Front*, p. 64 **L3** ❏ Biography, Literature, and Comparing Primary Sources booklet, *Navajo Code Talkers*, p. 30; *On Japanese American Internment*, p. 145 **L3** ❏ Exploring Primary Sources in U.S. History CD-ROM, *Rosie the Riveter Poster* **L3**

ASSESS/RETEACH	Targeted Resources
Monitor Progress Assess students' completed graphic organizers using the Section Reading Support Transparency. **Assess** Use the Section 5 Quiz to evaluate student understanding of key concepts in this section. **Reteach** Assign students the Guide to the Essentials.	❏ Section Reading Support Transparencies **L1** **ELL** ❏ Guided Reading and Review booklet, p. 104 **L1** ❏ Section 5 Quiz, Units 7/8 booklet, p. 64 **L1** **L2** ❏ Guide to the Essentials, p. 130 **L1** **L2** ❏ GoOnline: PHSchool.com, Chapter 25 Self-Test, Web Code: mra-8256 ❏ Chapter 25 Tests, Units 7/8 booklet, pp. 65, 68

Homework _____

_____

Key
L1 Basic to Average   **L3** Average to Advanced
L2 For All Students   **ELL** English Language Learners

LESSON PLAN 26.1
Origins of the Cold War
⏰ *1 Period, .5 Block*

Section Objectives

1. Learn why 1945 was a critical year in United States foreign relations.
2. Discover some of the postwar goals of the United States and the Soviet Union.
3. Find out how the iron curtain tightened the Soviet hold over Eastern Europe.
4. See how the Truman Doctrine complemented the policy of containment.

Local Standards

Vocabulary satellite nation • iron curtain • Cold War • containment • Truman Doctrine

---

FOCUS

Teach Key Concepts and Vocabulary
Ask students to identify the conflicting goals of the United States and the Soviet Union after World War II.

Build Background Knowledge
Remind students that the United States, a democratic country, and the Soviet Union, a Communist country, had a history of bad feelings. Even as wartime allies, they disagreed about battle tactics and long-term strategies.

Targeted Resources
❏ Activating Prior Knowledge, TE p. 868 **L1**
❏ Historical Outline Map Book, *Europe After World War II*, p. 68; *Europe*, p. 77 **L1**
❏ Sounds of an Era Audio CD, *"Iron Curtain Speech,"* Winston Churchill

---

INSTRUCT

Develop Understanding
Discuss with students how the Cold War developed, including Soviet expansion throughout Eastern Europe and American attempts to prevent the further spread of communism.

Monitor Comprehension
Have students discuss how the Truman Doctrine reflected the policy of containment.

Targeted Resources
❏ Skills for Life booklet, p. 28 **L1**
❏ Learning with Documents booklet, Uncle Joe, p. 31; *What They Fear Most*, p. 68 **L3**
❏ Biography, Literature, and Comparing Primary Sources booklet, *George F. Kennan*, p. 31 **L3**
❏ Prentice Hall U.S. History Video Collection, Vol. 20, Post-War USA

ASSESS/RETEACH

Monitor Progress
Assess students' completed graphic organizers using the Section Reading Support Transparency.

Assess
Use the Section 1 Quiz to evaluate student understanding of key concepts in this section.

Reteach
Assign students the section summary in the Guide to the Essentials.

Targeted Resources
❏ Section Reading Support Transparencies **L1** **ELL**
❏ Guided Reading and Review booklet, p. 105 **L1**
❏ Section 1 Quiz, Units 7/8 booklet, p. 72 **L1** **L2**
❏ Guide to the Essentials, p. 132 **L1** **L2**
❏ Social Studies Skills Tutor CD-ROM **L1**
❏ Guided Reading Audiotapes **ELL**

Homework _____

_____

Key
L1 Basic to Average   **L3** Average to Advanced
L2 For All Students   **ELL** English Language Learners

LESSON PLAN 26.2
The Cold War Heats Up
🕐 *1 Period, .5 Block*

Section Objectives

Local Standards

1. Find out how the Marshall Plan, the Berlin Airlift, and NATO helped to achieve American goals in postwar Europe.
2. Realize how Communist advances affected American foreign policy.
3. See how the Cold War affected American life at home.

Vocabulary Marshall Plan • Berlin airlift • North Atlantic Treaty Organization (NATO) • collective security • Warsaw Pact • House Un-American Activities Committee (HUAC) • Hollywood Ten • blacklist • McCarran-Walter Act

FOCUS

Targeted Resources

Teach Key Concepts and Vocabulary
Ask students to identify steps the United States took to strengthen postwar Europe economically and militarily, and have them describe how the Western Allies overcame the Soviet blockade of West Berlin.

❏ Activating Prior Knowledge, TE p. 876 **L1**

❏ Color Transparencies, Historical Maps, A45, A46 **L2**

❏ Sounds of an Era Audio CD, *George Marshall, June 5, 1947; President Truman, 1948; House Un-American Activities Committee Testimony, 1948*

Build Background Knowledge
Explain to students that the risk of a "shooting war" between the United States and the Soviet Union was high, especially in the first few years after World War II.

INSTRUCT

Targeted Resources

Develop Understanding
Discuss with students why the blockade of West Berlin is a prime example of how easily the Cold War could heat up.

Monitor Comprehension
Have students discuss how the threat of communism led to a renewed anti-Communist crusade in the United States.

❏ Learning Styles Lesson Plans booklet, p. 54 **L2**

❏ Biography, Literature, and Comparing Primary Sources booklet, *On Joining NATO*, pp. 147–148 **L3**

❏ Presentation Pro CD-ROM, Chapter 26, Section 2 **L1**

ASSESS/RETEACH

Targeted Resources

Monitor Progress
Assess students' completed graphic organizers using the Section Reading Support Transparency.

Assess
Use the Section 2 Quiz to evaluate student understanding of key concepts in this section.

Reteach
Assign students the Guide to the Essentials.

❏ Section Reading Support Transparencies **L1 ELL**

❏ Guided Reading and Review booklet, p. 106 **L1**

❏ Section 2 Quiz, Units 7/8 booklet, p. 73 **L1 L2**

❏ Guide to the Essentials, p. 133 **L1 L2**

❏ Guided Reading Audiotapes **ELL**

Homework _____

_____

Key
L1 Basic to Average   **L3** Average to Advanced
L2 For All Students   **ELL** English Language Learners

LESSON PLAN 26.3
The Korean War
🕐 *.5 Period, .25 Block*

Section Objectives

1. Observe the ways Communist expansion in Asia set the stage for the Korean War.
2. Learn who fought in the Korean War, and about the war's three stages.
3. Discover the different effects of the Korean War.

Vocabulary 38th parallel • Korean War • military-industrial complex

Local Standards

FOCUS

Teach Key Concepts and Vocabulary
Ask students to explain why the United States acted quickly to oppose the invasion of South Korea by North Korean troops in 1950.

Build Background Knowledge
Remind students that the policy of containment aimed to keep the Soviet Union from spreading communism to other nations, and the Truman Doctrine urged the United States to support nations threatened with communism.

Targeted Resources

❏ Activating Prior Knowledge, TE p. 884 **L1**
❏ Color Transparencies, Historical Maps, A47 **L2**
❏ Historical Outline Map Book, *The Korean War*, p. 69 **L1**
❏ Sounds of an Era Audio CD, *General Douglas MacArthur*, April 19, 1951

INSTRUCT

Develop Understanding
Discuss with students the course of the Korean War—how the United States, through the United Nations, helped repel the North Koreans, then fell back in the face of an onslaught of Chinese forces, and later settled for a truce at about the original dividing line between the two Koreas.

Monitor Comprehension
Ask students why President Truman fired General MacArthur.

Targeted Resources

❏ Learning with Documents booklet, *General Douglas MacArthur, Address to Congress*, p. 89 **L3**
❏ Presentation Pro CD-ROM, Chapter 26, Section 3 **L1**

ASSESS/RETEACH

Monitor Progress
Assess students' completed graphic organizers using the Section Reading Support Transparency. Review the answers to the Guided Reading and Review worksheet.

Assess
Use the Section 3 Quiz to evaluate student understanding of key concepts in this section.

Reteach
Assign students the Guide to the Essentials.

Homework _____

_____

Targeted Resources

❏ Section Reading Support Transparencies **L1** **ELL**
❏ Guided Reading and Review booklet, p. 107 **L1**
❏ Section 3 Quiz, Units 7/8 booklet, p. 74 **L1** **L2**
❏ Guide to the Essentials, p. 134 **L1** **L2**
❏ Guided Reading Audiotapes **ELL**
❏ Student Edition on Audio CD **ELL**

Key
L1 Basic to Average   **L3** Average to Advanced
L2 For All Students   **ELL** English Language Learners

LESSON PLAN 26.4

The Continuing Cold War

🕐 .5 Period, .25 Block

Section Objectives

1. Discover some characteristics of the McCarthy era.
2. See how the Cold War was waged in Southeast Asia, the Middle East, and Latin America during the 1950s.
3. Understand how the arms race developed.

Vocabulary McCarthyism • arms race • deterrence • brinkmanship • ICBM • *Sputnik* • U-2 incident

Local Standards

FOCUS

Teach Key Concepts and Vocabulary
Ask students to describe how the Cold War was waged in the 1950s.

Build Background Knowledge
Remind students that the United States aimed to oppose the expansion of Soviet influence and the spread of communism wherever they occurred.

Targeted Resources

❏ Activating Prior Knowledge, TE p. 889 **L1**
❏ Color Transparencies, Political Cartoons, B14; *Cause-and-Effect Charts*, D10 **L2**
❏ Historical Outline Map Book, *The Middle East*, p. 78 **L1**
❏ Sounds of an Era Audio CD, *Army-McCarthy Hearings, 1954; Eisenhower's Farewell Address*, 1961

INSTRUCT

Develop Understanding
Discuss with students how America's military strategy during the Cold War differed from that of World War II, partly in response to the new availability of nuclear weapons.

Monitor Comprehension
Ask students how the Israeli-Palestinian conflict first got started and what role the United States and the Soviet Union played.

Targeted Resources

❏ Learning Styles Lesson Plans booklet, p. 55 **L2**
❏ Biography, Literature, and Comparing Primary Sources booklet, *The Ugly American*, p. 75 **L3**
❏ Presentation Pro CD-ROM, Chapter 26, Section 4 **L1**

ASSESS/RETEACH

Monitor Progress
Assess students' completed graphic organizers using the Section Reading Support Transparency. Review the answers to the Guided Reading and Review worksheet.

Assess
Use the Section 4 Quiz to evaluate student understanding of key concepts in this section.

Reteach
Assign students the section summary in the Guide to the Essentials

Targeted Resources

❏ Section Reading Support Transparencies **L1** **ELL**
❏ Guided Reading and Review booklet, p. 108 **L1**
❏ Section 4 Quiz, Units 7/8 booklet, p. 75 **L1** **L2**
❏ Guide to the Essentials, p. 135 **L1** **L2**
❏ Chapter Summary, Units 7/8 booklet, p. 71 **L1** **ELL**
❏ GoOnline: PHSchool.com, Chapter 26 Self-Test, Web Code: mra-8265
❏ Chapter 26 Tests, Units 7/8 booklet, pp. 76, 79

Homework _____

_____

Key
L1 Basic to Average   **L3** Average to Advanced
L2 For All Students   **ELL** English Language Learners

LESSON PLAN 27.1

The Postwar Economy

1 Period, .5 Block

Section Objectives

1. Find out how businesses reorganized after World War II.
2. Learn how technology transformed life after World War II.
3. Discover ways in which the nation's workforce changed after World War II.
4. See how suburbs and highway systems grew after World War II.
5. Understand how postwar conditions affected consumer credit.

Local Standards

Vocabulary per capita income • conglomerate • franchise • transistor • baby boom • GI Bill of Rights

FOCUS

Teach Key Concepts and Vocabulary
Ask students how the economic boom after World War II changed American life.

Build Background Knowledge
Explain that Americans came out of World War II full of hope for the future. The war had ended the Depression, the economy was starting to expand, and Americans were in a mood to spend.

Targeted Resources
- ❑ Activating Prior Knowledge, TE p. 900 **L1**
- ❑ Color Transparencies, *Political Cartoons*, B15 **L2**
- ❑ Sounds of an Era Audio CD, *"Route 66,"* Nat King Cole Trio

INSTRUCT

Develop Understanding
Discuss why the economy expanded. Ask students to describe advances in business organization and in technology.

Monitor Comprehension
Ask students how advances in medicine contributed to the postwar spirit of optimism.

Targeted Resources
- ❑ Learning with Documents booklet, *The Miracle of Television*, p. 66 **L3**
- ❑ Exploring Primary Sources in U.S. History CD-ROM, *Dr. Salk and His Vaccine* **L9**
- ❑ Prentice Hall U.S. History Video Collection, Vol. 20, Postwar USA

ASSESS/RETEACH

Monitor Progress
Assess students' completed graphic organizers using the Section Reading Support Transparency.

Assess
Use the Section 1 Quiz to evaluate student understanding of key concepts in this section.

Reteach
Assign students the Guide to the Essentials.

Targeted Resources
- ❑ Section Reading Support Transparencies **L1** **ELL**
- ❑ Guided Reading and Review booklet, p. 109 **L1**
- ❑ Section 1 Quiz, Units 7/8 booklet, p. 83 **L1** **L2**
- ❑ Guide to the Essentials, p. 137 **L1** **L2**
- ❑ Guided Reading Audiotapes **ELL**

Homework _____

_____

Key
L1 Basic to Average	**L3** Average to Advanced
L2 For All Students	**ELL** English Language Learners

LESSON PLAN 27.2
The Mood of the 1950s
⏲ .5 Period, .25 Block

Section Objectives
1. Find out why comfort and security were so important to Americans in the 1950s.
2. Learn about the accepted roles of men and women during the 1950s.
3. See how some people challenged conformity in the 1950s.

Vocabulary rock-and-roll • beatnik

Local Standards

FOCUS

Teach Key Concepts and Vocabulary
Ask students whether they think the prosperity and security that Americans felt in the 1950s was worth the price of conformity.

Build Background Knowledge
Explain to students that Americans conformed with expected roles and behaviors in part because they treasured their new prosperity and security and did not want to "rock the boat."

Targeted Resources
❏ Activating Prior Knowledge, TE p. 907 **L1**
❏ Sounds of an Era Audio CD, *The Feminine Mystique,* Betty Friedan; "Hand Clappin'," Red Prysock

INSTRUCT

Develop Understanding
Discuss how people behave when they want to fit into a group. Ask students for examples of this kind of conforming behavior in Americans of the 1950s.

Monitor Comprehension
Ask students how rock-and-roll and the beatniks challenged the conformity of the 1950s.

Targeted Resources
❏ Learning Styles Lesson Plans booklet, p. 57 **L2**
❏ Biography, Literature, and Comparing Primary Sources booklet, *On Rock and Roll,* pp. 149–150 **L3**
❏ Presentation Pro CD-ROM, Chapter 27, Section 2 **L1**

ASSESS/RETEACH

Monitor Progress
Assess students' completed graphic organizers using the Section Reading Support Transparency. Review the answers to the Guided Reading and Review worksheet.

Assess
Use the Section 2 Quiz to evaluate student understanding of key concepts in this section.

Reteach
Assign students the section summary in the Guide to the Essentials.

Targeted Resources
❏ Section Reading Support Transparencies **L1** **ELL**
❏ Guided Reading and Review booklet, p. 110 **L1**
❏ Section 2 Quiz, Units 7/8 booklet, p. 84 **L1 L2**
❏ Guide to the Essentials, p. 138 **L1 L2**
❏ Guided Reading Audiotapes **ELL**
❏ Student Edition on Audio CD **ELL**

Homework _____

_____

Key
L1 Basic to Average   **L3** Average to Advanced
L2 For All Students   **ELL** English Language Learners

LESSON PLAN 27.3

Domestic Politics and Policy

🕐 *1 Period, .5 Block*

Section Objectives | Local Standards

1. Discover Truman's domestic policies as outlined in the Fair Deal.
2. Learn how Truman won the ‚ection of 1948.
3. Understand the Republican approach to government during the Eisenhower presidency.

Vocabulary reconversion • Taft-Hartley Act • Modern Republicanism • National Aeronautics and Space Administration (NASA) • National Defense Education Act

| **FOCUS** | **Targeted Resources** |

Teach Key Concepts and Vocabulary
Ask students to explain how Truman and Eisenhower disagreed about the proper role of government and about how to solve the nation's postwar social problems.

❏ Activating Prior Knowledge, TE p. 912 **L1**
❏ Sounds of an Era Audio CD, *"The Checkers Speech,"* Richard Nixon

Build Background Knowledge
Remind students that Truman was a Democrat and Eisenhower was a Republican. Like his predecessor, Franklin Roosevelt, Truman believed that government should play an active role in the economy.

| **INSTRUCT** | **Targeted Resources** |

Develop Understanding
Discuss whether Truman or Eisenhower had greater success in returning the nation to stability.

Monitor Comprehension
Ask students to compare the Fair Deal with the New Deal and with Modern Republicanism.

❏ Skills for Life booklet, p. 29 **L1**
❏ Learning with Documents booklet, *Enforcing Brown v. Board of Education,* p. 32 **L3**
❏ Biography, Literature, and Comparing Primary Sources booklet, *Conformity in the 1950s,* pp. 76–77 **L3**

| **ASSESS/RETEACH** | **Targeted Resources** |

Monitor Progress
Assess students' completed graphic organizers using the Section Reading Support Transparency. Review the answers to the Guided Reading and Review worksheet.

Assess
Use the Section 3 Quiz to evaluate student understanding of key concepts in this section.

Reteach
Assign students the section summary in the Guide to the Essentials.

❏ Section Reading Support Transparencies **L1** **ELL**
❏ Guided Reading and Review booklet, p. 111 **L1**
❏ Section 3 Quiz, Units 7/8 booklet, p. 85 **L1** **L2**
❏ Guide to the Essentials, p. 139 **L1** **L2**
❏ Chapter Summary, Units 7/8 booklet, p. 82 **L1** **ELL**
❏ GoOnline: PHSchool.com, Chapter 27 Self-Test, Web Code: mra-8274
❏ Chapter 27 Tests, Units 7/8 booklet, pp. 86, 89

Homework _____
_____

Key
L1 Basic to Average   **L3** Average to Advanced
L2 For All Students   **ELL** English Language Learners

LESSON PLAN 28.1
Demands for Civil Rights Movement
🕐 *1 Period, .5 Block*

Section Objectives
1. Learn about events and cultural trends that led to a rise in African American influence in the twentieth century.
2. Find out how Americans responded to the Supreme Court's decision in *Brown* v. *Board of Education*.
3. Discover how the Montgomery bus boycott affected the civil rights movement.
4. See how other minorities began to demand civil rights in the 1960s.

Local Standards

Vocabulary *Brown* v. *Board of Education of Topeka, Kansas* • Montgomery bus boycott • integration

FOCUS

Teach Key Concepts and Vocabulary
Ask students to explain why the time was right in 1954 for the Supreme Court to integrate public schools.

Build Background Knowledge
Remind students that segregation was still legal in the early postwar years, but that a confluence of social, economic, and demographic conditions paved the way for civil rights advances.

Targeted Resources
❏ Activating Prior Knowledge, TE p. 930 **L1**
❏ Sounds of an Era Audio CD, Reaction to *Brown* v. *Board of Education*, 1954

INSTRUCT

Develop Understanding
Discuss *Plessy* v. *Ferguson* and the historic *Brown* ruling that overturned it. Have students describe the public's reaction to the Supreme Court's decision, including the Arkansas governor's defiance at a Little Rock high school.

Monitor Comprehension
Ask students to identify the results of the Montgomery bus boycott.

Targeted Resources
❏ Learning with Documents booklet, Enforcing *Brown* v. *Board of Education*, p. 33; *Brown* v. *Board of Education*, p. 92 **L3**
❏ Biography, Literature, and Comparing Primary Sources booklet, *Thurgood Marshall*, p. 33 **L3**
❏ American Heritage, My Brush With History, *Encounters With Segregation*, Student Edition pp. 962–963, Videotape

ASSESS/RETEACH

Monitor Progress
Assess students' completed graphic organizers using the Section Reading Support Transparency.

Assess
Use the Section 1 Quiz to evaluate student understanding of key concepts in this section.

Reteach
Assign students the Guide to the Essentials.

Targeted Resources
❏ Section Reading Support Transparencies **L1** **ELL**
❏ Guided Reading and Review booklet, p. 112 **L1**
❏ Section 1 Quiz, Units 9/10 booklet, p. 4 **L1** **L2**
❏ Guide to the Essentials, p. 141 **L1** **L2**

Homework _____
_____

Key
L1 Basic to Average **L3** Average to Advanced
L2 For All Students **ELL** English Language Learners

LESSON PLAN 28.2
Leaders and Strategies

.5 Period, .25 Block

Section Objectives

1. Find out how early groups laid the foundation for the civil rights movement.
2. Understand the philosophy of nonviolence.
3. Realize how SNCC gave students a voice in the civil rights movement.

Local Standards

Vocabulary interracial • Congress of Racial Equality (CORE) • Southern Christian Leadership Conference (SCLC) • nonviolent protest • Student Nonviolent Coordinating Committee (SNCC)

FOCUS

Teach Key Concepts and Vocabulary
Ask students to describe the differences among civil rights organizations, as well as the ways in which they were united.

Build Background Knowledge
Explain to students that the civil rights movement was not a monolithic organization under the sway of a single leader, but rather a diverse group of organizations and people.

Targeted Resources

❑ Activating Prior Knowledge, TE p. 936 **L1**

INSTRUCT

Develop Understanding
Discuss the first quotation by Martin Luther King, Jr., under the heading "A New Voice for Students." Ask students whether they agree with King's statements, especially as they related to the fight for civil rights.

Monitor Comprehension
Ask students how the inclusion of students affected the civil rights movement.

Targeted Resources

❑ Learning with Documents booklet, *Nonviolent Resistance*, p. 67 **L3**
❑ Biography, Literature, and Comparing Primary Sources booklet, *On School Integration*, pp. 151–152; *SNCC Workers*, pp. 78–79 **L3**
❑ Presentation Pro CD-ROM, Chapter 28, Section 2 **L1**

ASSESS/RETEACH

Monitor Progress
Assess students' completed graphic organizers using the Section Reading Support Transparency. Review the answers to the Guided Reading and Review worksheet.

Assess
Use the Section 2 Quiz to evaluate student understanding of key concepts in this section.

Reteach
Assign students the section summary in the Guide to the Essentials.

Targeted Resources

❑ Section Reading Support Transparencies **L1** **ELL**
❑ Guided Reading and Review booklet, p. 113 **L1**
❑ Section 2 Quiz, Units 9/10 booklet, p. 5 **L1** **L2**
❑ Guide to the Essentials, p. 142 **L1** **L2**
❑ Guided Reading Audiotapes **ELL**
❑ Student Edition on Audio CD **ELL**

Homework _____
_____

Key
L1 Basic to Average   **L3** Average to Advanced
L2 For All Students   **ELL** English Language Learners

LESSON PLAN 28.3

The Struggle Intensifies

🕐 *1 Period, .5 Block*

Section Objectives	**Local Standards**

1. Identify the goals of sit-ins and Freedom Rides.
2. Find out the reaction to James Meredith's integration at the University of Mississippi.
3. Understand how the events in Birmingham, Alabama, affected the nation's attitudes toward the civil rights movement.

Vocabulary sit-in • Freedom Ride

FOCUS

Teach Key Concepts and Vocabulary
Ask students to describe what happened as a result of the protests against segregation that began to sweep the South.

Build Background Knowledge
Remind students that protests such as sit-ins, boycotts, and marches remained largely nonviolent, despite the often violent reactions they aroused.

Targeted Resources
❑ Activating Prior Knowledge, TE p. 941 **L1**
❑ Color Transparencies, *American Photo*, F9; *Political Cartoons*, B16 **L2**
❑ Sounds of an Era Audio CD, *A Sit-in in Nashville, Tennessee*

INSTRUCT

Develop Understanding
Discuss with students the issues that made the civil rights movement so unstoppable, including the tactics, moral philosophy, and leaders of the movement.

Monitor Comprehension
Ask students how the government responded when Freedom Riders faced violent opposition in the South.

Targeted Resources
❑ Learning Styles Lesson Plans booklet, p. 59 **L2**
❑ Skills for Life booklet, p. 30 L1
❑ Learning with Documents booklet, *Protecting the Freedom Riders*, p. 33 **L3**
❑ Presentation Pro CD-ROM, Chapter 28, Section 3 **L1**
❑ Exploring Primary Sources in U.S. History CD-ROM, *Letter from Birmingham Jail, Martin Luther King, Jr.* **L3**

ASSESS/RETEACH

Monitor Progress
Assess students' completed graphic organizers using the Section Reading Support Transparency.

Assess
Use the Section 3 Quiz to evaluate student understanding of key concepts in this section.

Reteach
Assign students the section summary in the Guide to the Essentials.

Targeted Resources
❑ Section Reading Support Transparencies **L1** **ELL**
❑ Guided Reading and Review booklet, p. 114 **L1**
❑ Section 3 Quiz, Units 9/10 booklet, p. 6 **L1** **L2**
❑ Guide to the Essentials, p. 143 **L1** **L2**
❑ Social Studies Skills Tutor CD-ROM **L1**
❑ Guided Reading Audiotapes **ELL**
❑ Student Edition on Audio CD **ELL**

Homework _____

_____

Key
L1 Basic to Average   **L3** Average to Advanced
L2 For All Students   **ELL** English Language Learners

LESSON PLAN 28.4
The Political Response
1 Period, .5 Block

Section Objectives

Local Standards

1. Learn about President Kennedy's approach to civil rights.
2. Find out why civil rights leaders proposed a march on Washington.
3. Learn the goals of the Civil Rights Act of 1964.
4. Discover how African Americans fought to gain voting rights.

Vocabulary March on Washington • filibuster • cloture • Civil Rights Act of 1964 • Voting Rights Act of 1965 • Twenty-fourth Amendment

FOCUS

Targeted Resources

Teach Key Concepts and Vocabulary
Ask students to explain why politicians such as President Kennedy began taking a strong stand for civil rights in the 1960s.

❏ Activating Prior Knowledge, TE p. 948 **L1**
❏ Sounds of an Era Audio CD, *"I Have a Dream," Martin Luther King, Jr.*

Build Background Knowledge
Explain that Kennedy and other Democrats had been reluctant to alienate Southerners, who tended to vote Democratic but also favored segregation. By the 1960s, as Kennedy found out, African Americans had also begun to gain political clout.

INSTRUCT

Targeted Resources

Develop Understanding
Discuss the different ways that Kennedy and Johnson promoted the passage of civil rights legislation. Ask students which President they think was more successful and why.

❏ Learning with Documents booklet, *Martin Luther King, Jr., "I Have a Dream,"* p. 91 **L3**
❏ Presentation Pro CD-ROM, Chapter 28, Section 4 **L1**
❏ Exploring Primary Sources in U.S. History CD-ROM, *I Have a Dream, Martin Luther King, Jr.; Reynolds v. Sims* **L3**

Monitor Comprehension
Ask students why the Civil Rights Act of 1964 and the Voting Rights Act of 1965 were so important to African Americans in the South.

ASSESS/RETEACH

Targeted Resources

Monitor Progress
Assess students' completed graphic organizers using the Section Reading Support Transparency.

❏ Section Reading Support Transparencies **L1** **ELL**

Assess
Use the Section 4 Quiz to evaluate student understanding of key concepts in this section.

❏ Guided Reading and Review booklet, p. 115 **L1**
❏ Section 4 Quiz, Units 9/10 booklet, p. 7 **L1** **L2**
❏ Guide to the Essentials, p. 144 **L1** **L2**

Reteach
Assign students the Guide to the Essentials.

Homework _____
_____

Key
L1 Basic to Average
L2 For All Students
L3 Average to Advanced
ELL English Language Learners

LESSON PLAN 28.5

The Movement Takes a New Turn

🕐 *1 Period, .5 Block*

Section Objectives

1. Learn about Malcolm X's approach to gaining civil rights.
2. Become familiar with the major goals of the black power movement.
3. See why violent riots erupted in many urban streets.
4. Find out how the tragic events of 1968 affected the nation.

Vocabulary Nation of Islam • black nationalism • black power • de jure segregation • de facto segregation

Local Standards

FOCUS

Teach Key Concepts and Vocabulary
Ask students to describe the reactions of some African Americans who grew angry at the slow pace of change in the area of civil rights.

Build Background Knowledge
Explain that the civil rights acts passed in the mid-1960s took time to implement and that meanwhile, economic and social discrimination against African Americans continued.

Targeted Resources
❏ Activating Prior Knowledge, TE p. 954 **L1**
❏ Sounds of an Era Audio CD, *Report of Robert Kennedy Assassination*

INSTRUCT

Develop Understanding
Discuss the various alternatives to nonviolent confrontation that evolved in the civil rights movement.

Monitor Comprehension
Ask students to explain the role that de facto segregation played in the riots that broke out in several cities during the 1960s.

Targeted Resources
❏ Presentation Pro CD-ROM, Chapter 28, Section 5 **L1**

ASSESS/RETEACH

Monitor Progress
Assess students' completed graphic organizers using the Section Reading Support Transparency. Review the answers to the Guided Reading and Review worksheet.

Assess
Use the Section 5 Quiz to evaluate student understanding of key concepts in this section.

Reteach
Assign students the Guide to the Essentials.

Targeted Resources
❏ Section Reading Support Transparencies **L1** **ELL**
❏ Guided Reading and Review booklet, p. 116 **L1**
❏ Section 5 Quiz, Units 9/10 booklet, p. 8 **L1** **L2**
❏ Guide to the Essentials, p. 145 **L1** **L2**
❏ GoOnline: PHSchool.com, Chapter 28 Self-Test, Web Code: mra-9286
❏ Chapter 28 Tests, Units 9/10 booklet, pp. 9, 12

Homework _____

_____

Key
L1 Basic to Average   **L3** Average to Advanced
L2 For All Students   **ELL** English Language Learners

LESSON PLAN 29.1
The New Frontier
⏱ *1 Period, .5 Block*

Section Objectives

1. Learn about factors that affected the election of 1960.
2. Find out about domestic programs pursued by President Kennedy.
3. Read about circumstances that surrounded Kennedy's assassination.

Local Standards

Vocabulary mandate • New Frontier • Warren Commission

FOCUS

Teach Key Concepts and Vocabulary
Ask students to explain why so few of Kennedy's proposed new programs made it through Congress.

Build Background Knowledge
Remind students that Kennedy's narrow victory in the presidential election left him without a mandate.

Targeted Resources

❏ Activating Prior Knowledge, TE p. 968 **L1**
❏ Sounds of an Era Audio CD, President John F. *Kennedy's Inaugural Address*, 1961; *Walter Cronkite on Kennedy's Death*, 1963; *A Dallas Reporter on Kennedy's Assassination*; "*A Taste of Honey*" **L3**

INSTRUCT

Develop Understanding
Discuss Kennedy's New Frontier, including proposals to boost the ailing economy, help the poor, and revive the space program.

Monitor Comprehension
Ask students what the Warren Commission concluded about Kennedy's assassination.

Targeted Resources

❏ Learning Styles Lesson Plans booklet, p. 60 **L2**
❏ Skills for Life booklet, p. 31 **L1**
❏ Learning with Documents booklet, *Close Allies*, p. 68 **L3**
❏ Biography, Literature, and Comparing Primary Sources booklet, *A Grieving Nation*, p. 80 **L3**
❏ Exploring Primary Sources in U.S. History CD-ROM, *Colonel Glenn Rides into Space* **L3**
❏ Prentice Hall U.S. History Video Collection, Vol. 20, *Post-War USA*

ASSESS/RETEACH

Monitor Progress
Assess students' completed graphic organizers using the Section Reading Support Transparency.

Assess
Use the Section 1 Quiz to evaluate student understanding of key concepts in this section.

Reteach
Assign students the Guide to the Essentials.

Targeted Resources

❏ Section Reading Support Transparencies **L1** **ELL**
❏ Guided Reading and Review booklet, p. 117 **L1**
❏ Section 1 Quiz, Units 3/4 booklet, p. 16 **L1** **L2**
❏ Guide to the Essentials, p. 147 **L1** **L2**

Homework _____
_____

Key
L1 Basic to Average   **L3** Average to Advanced
L2 For All Students   **ELL** English Language Learners

LESSON PLAN 29.2
The Great Society
1 Period, .5 Block

Section Objectives

1. Discover Lyndon Johnson's path to the presidency.
2. Find out about some of the goals and programs of the Great Society.
3. Learn about some of the cases that made the Warren Court both important and controversial.

Vocabulary Great Society • Head Start • Volunteers in Service to America (VISTA) • Medicare • Medicaid • Immigration Act of 1965 • Miranda rule • apportionment

Local Standards

FOCUS

Teach Key Concepts and Vocabulary
Ask students to identify Johnson's most important reform bills and summarize their goals.

Build Background Knowledge
Explain to students that Johnson witnessed poverty as a school teacher in Texas, and his concern for the poor led him into politics.

Targeted Resources

❏ Activating Prior Knowledge, TE p. 975 **L1**
❏ Color Transparencies, *Political Cartoons*, B17 **L2**
❏ Sounds of an Era Audio CD, *"The Times They Are A-Changing,"* Bob Dylan; *Great Society Speech*, 1964 **L3**

INSTRUCT

Develop Understanding
Discuss with students how Johnson was able to push such a broad array of legislation through Congress.

Monitor Comprehension
Ask students to identify some of the landmark cases handed down by the Warren Court.

Targeted Resources

❏ Learning with Documents booklet, *President Johnson's Thanksgiving Address*, p. 34; Lyndon B. Johnson, *The Great Society*, p. 94 **L3**
❏ Presentation Pro CD-ROM, Chapter 29, Section 2 **L1**

ASSESS/RETEACH

Monitor Progress
Assess students' completed graphic organizers using the Section Reading Support Transparency. Review the answers to the Guided Reading and Review worksheet.

Assess
Use the Section 2 Quiz to evaluate student understanding of key concepts in this section.

Reteach
Assign students the section summary in the Guide to the Essentials.

Targeted Resources

❏ Section Reading Support Transparency **L1** **ELL**
❏ Guided Reading and Review booklet, p. 39 **L1**
❏ Section 2 Quiz, Unit 3/4 booklet, p. 28 **L1** **L2**
❏ Guide to the Essentials, p. 49 **L1** **L2**
❏ Social Studies Skills Tutor CD-ROM **L1**
❏ Guided Reading Audiotapes **ELL**
❏ Student Edition on Audio CD **ELL**

Homework _____

_____

Key
L1 Basic to Average   **L3** Average to Advanced
L2 For All Students   **ELL** English Language Learners

LESSON PLAN 29.3

Foreign Policy in the Early 1960s

🕐 *1 Period, .5 Block*

Section Objectives

1. Understand the goals and the outcome of the Bay of Pigs invasion.
2. Read to find out about events that led to the Berlin Crisis and the Cuban Missile Crisis.
3. Discover the goals of the Alliance for Progress and the Peace Corps.
4. Find out about Cold War conflicts in which Johnson became involved.

Vocabulary Bay of Pigs invasion • Berlin Wall • Cuban Missile Crisis • Limited Test Ban Treaty • Alliance for Progress • Peace Corps

Local Standards

FOCUS

Teach Key Concepts and Vocabulary
Ask students to explain how Kennedy and Johnson responded to challenges during the Cold War.

Build Background Knowledge
Remind students that the existence of nuclear missiles in the hands of both superpowers added tension to every Cold War crisis.

Targeted Resources
❏ Activating Prior Knowledge, TE p. 983 **L1**
❏ Color Transparencies, Historical Maps, A48, A49; *The Way It Works,* H19 **L2**

INSTRUCT

Develop Understanding
Have students make a time line of events during the Cuban Missile Crisis and then use the time line to discuss the crisis. Ask students to pinpoint the most critical time period.

Monitor Comprehension
Ask students to explain the underlying political goal of the Alliance for Progress and the Peace Corps.

Targeted Resources
❏ Learning Styles Lesson Plans booklet, p. 61 **L2**
❏ Learning with Documents booklet, John F. Kennedy, *Inaugural Address,* p. 93 **L3**
❏ Biography, Literature, and Comparing Primary Sources booklet, *Robert F. Kennedy,* p. 34; *On the Cold War,* p. 153 **L3**
❏ Exploring Primary Sources in U.S. History CD-ROM, *On the Cuban Missile Crisis,* John F. Kennedy and Nikita Khrushchev **L3**

ASSESS/RETEACH

Monitor Progress
Assess students' completed graphic organizers using the Section Reading Support Transparency. Review the answers to the Guided Reading and Review worksheet.

Assess
Use the Section 3 Quiz to evaluate student understanding of key concepts in this section.

Reteach
Assign students the Guide to the Essentials.

Targeted Resources
❏ Section Reading Support Transparency **ELL**
❏ Guided Reading and Review booklet, p. 119 **L1**
❏ Section 3 Quiz, Units 9/10 booklet, p. 18 **L1** **L2**
❏ Guide to the Essentials, p. 149 **L1** **L2**
❏ GoOnline: PHSchool.com, Chapter 29 Self-Test, Web Code: mra-9294
❏ Chapter 29 Tests, Units 9/10, pp. 19, 22

Homework _____

_____

Key
L1 Basic to Average
L2 For All Students
L3 Average to Advanced
ELL English Language Learners

LESSON PLAN 30.1

The Women's Movement

🕐 *1 Period, .5 Block*

Section Objectives	**Local Standards**

Section Objectives

1. Discover the background of the women's movement.
2. Find out how women organized to gain support and to effect change.
3. Observe the impact of feminism.
4. Learn which groups opposed the women's movement and why.

Vocabulary feminism • National Organization for Women (NOW) • *Roe* v. *Wade* • Equal Rights Amendment (ERA)

FOCUS

Teach Key Concepts and Vocabulary
Ask students to explain how the women's movement affected American society.

Build Background Knowledge
Remind students that women's movement looked to the civil rights movement for inspiration and for strategies.

Targeted Resources

❏ Activating Prior Knowledge, TE p. 996 **L1**
❏ Color Transparencies, Fine Art, E20 **L2**
❏ Sounds of an Era Audio CD, *Bella Abzug on the ERA*, 1970 **L3**

INSTRUCT

Develop Understanding
Discuss the conditions in American society that led women to organize for change.

Monitor Comprehension
Have students discuss the Equal Rights Amendment and why it provoked such strong opposition.

Targeted Resources

❏ Learning with Documents booklet, *The Equal Rights Amendment*, p. 35 **L3**
❏ Biography, Literature, and Comparing Primary Sources booklet, *On Working Mothers*, pp. 155–156 **L3**
❏ Exploring Primary Sources in U.S. History CD-ROM, *Debate on the Equal Rights Amendment*, Representatives Emmanuel Celler and Edith Green **L3**
❏ Prentice Hall U.S. History Video Collection, Vol. 20, *Post-War USA*

ASSESS/RETEACH

Monitor Progress
Assess students' completed graphic organizers using the Section Reading Support Transparency.

Assess
Use the Section 1 Quiz to evaluate student understanding of key concepts in this section.

Reteach
Assign students the section summary in the Guide to the Essentials.

Targeted Resources

❏ Section Reading Support Transparencies **L1** **ELL**
❏ Guided Reading and Review booklet, p. 120 **L1**
❏ Section 1 Quiz, Units 9/10 booklet, p. 26 **L1** **L2**
❏ Guide to the Essentials, p. 151 **L1** **L2**

Homework _____

_____

Key
L1 Basic to Average
L2 For All Students
L3 Average to Advanced
ELL English Language Learners

LESSON PLAN 30.2
Ethnic Minorities Seek Equality
1 Period, .5 Block

Section Objectives

1. Learn how Latinos sought equality during the 1960s and early 1970s.
2. Find out how Asian Americans fought discrimination during this period.
3. See the ways in which Native Americans confronted their unique problems.

Local Standards

Vocabulary Latino • migrant farm worker • United Farm Workers (UFW) • Japanese American Citizens League (JACL) • American Indian Movement (AIM) • autonomy

---

FOCUS

Teach Key Concepts and Vocabulary
Ask students to explain how the Latino, Asian American, and Native American struggles for equality differed.

Build Background Knowledge
Explain to students that each minority cultural group has sought to have access to the same opportunities as the majority (Anglo or white) culture.

Targeted Resources
❏ Activating Prior Knowledge, TE p. 1003 **L1**
❏ Color Transparencies, *American Diversity*, G12 **L2**
❏ Sounds of an Era Audio CD, *César Chávez, 1973* **L3**

INSTRUCT

Develop Understanding
Discuss how Mexican Americans, or Chicanos, have organized against discrimination and gained political power.

Monitor Comprehension
Ask students to explain how the goals and tactics of the American Indian Movement differed from those of Latino and Asian American activists.

Targeted Resources
❏ Biography, Literature, and Comparing Primary Sources booklet, *Dolores Huerta*, p. 35; *Native American Voices*, p. 82 **L3**
❏ Presentation Pro CD-ROM, Chapter 30, Section 2 **L1**

ASSESS/RETEACH

Monitor Progress
Assess students' completed graphic organizers using the Section Reading Support Transparency. Review the answers to the Guided Reading and Review worksheet.

Assess
Use the Section 2 Quiz to evaluate student understanding of key concepts in this section.

Reteach
Assign students the section summary in the Guide to the Essentials.

Targeted Resources
❏ Section Reading Support Transparencies **L1** **ELL**
❏ Guided Reading and Review booklet, p. 121 **L1**
❏ Section 2 Quiz, Units 9/10 booklet, p. 27 **L1** **L2**
❏ Guide to the Essentials, p. 152 **L1** **L2**
❏ Guided Reading Audiotapes **ELL**
❏ Student Edition on Audio CD **ELL**

Homework _____

_____

Key
L1 Basic to Average   **L3** Average to Advanced
L2 For All Students   **ELL** English Language Learners

LESSON PLAN 30.3
The Counterculture
🕐 *.5 Period, .25 Block*

Section Objectives

1. Find out about social changes promoted by the counterculture.
2. Learn how the music world of the 1960s and 1970s contributed to the cultural changes of this era.

Vocabulary counterculture • Woodstock festival

Local Standards

FOCUS

Teach Key Concepts and Vocabulary
Ask students to explain how the counterculture affected American life in the 1960s and 1970s.

Build Background Knowledge
Remind students that the 1950s are often characterized as an era of conformity with traditional norms and values.

Targeted Resources

❑ Activating Prior Knowledge, TE p. 1009 **L1**

INSTRUCT

Develop Understanding
Discuss with students the values of the members of the counterculture, or hippies. Ask students to try to connect those values with the elements of mainstream American life that the hippies rejected.

Monitor Comprehension
Ask students to identify aspects of the counterculture that some people considered dangerous.

Targeted Resources

❑ Learning Styles Lesson Plans booklet, p. 62 **L2**

❑ Presentation Pro CD-ROM, Chapter 30, Section 3 **L1**

ASSESS/RETEACH

Monitor Progress
Assess students' completed graphic organizers using the Section Reading Support Transparency. Review the answers to the Guided Reading and Review worksheet.

Assess
Use the Section 3 Quiz to evaluate student understanding of key concepts in this section.

Reteach
Assign students the section summary in the Guide to the Essentials.

Targeted Resources

❑ Section Reading Support Transparencies **L1** **ELL**

❑ Guided Reading and Review booklet, p. 122 **L1**

❑ Section 3 Quiz, Units 9/10 booklet, p. 28 **L1** **L2**

❑ Guide to the Essentials, p. 153 **L1** **L2**

❑ Guided Reading Audiotapes **ELL**

❑ Student Edition on Audio CD **ELL**

Homework _____
_____

Key
L1 Basic to Average   **L3** Average to Advanced
L2 For All Students   **ELL** English Language Learners

LESSON PLAN 30.4

The Environmental and Consumer Movements

⏱ .5 Period, .25 Block

Section Objectives	**Local Standards**

Section Objectives

1. Read about efforts begun in the 1960s to protect the environment.
2. Understand how the government tried to balance jobs and environmental protection.
3. Find out how the consumer movement began, and what it tried to accomplish.

Vocabulary Nuclear Regulatory Commission (NRC) • Environmental Protection Agency (EPA) • Clean Air Act • Clean Water Act

---

FOCUS

Teach Key Concepts and Vocabulary

Ask students how successful the environmental and consumer movements were.

Build Background Knowledge

Explain that many environmental problems grew out of the rapid development of technology, industry, and transportation after World War II.

Targeted Resources

❏ Activating Prior Knowledge, TE p. 1013 **L1**
❏ Color Transparencies, *The Way It Works*, H20 **L2**
❏ Sounds of an Era Audio CD, *Rachel Carson on Silent Spring*, 1963; *Ralph Nader to the National Press Club*, 1966 **L3**

INSTRUCT

Develop Understanding

Ask students what role they think the federal government should play in regulating pollution and consumer safety.

Monitor Comprehension

Ask students to explain why Rachel Carson and Ralph Nader might be seen as pioneers.

Targeted Resources

❏ Learning Styles Lesson Plans booklet, p. 63 **L2**
❏ Learning with Documents booklet, *Preserving the Environment*, p. 69 **L3**
❏ Presentation Pro CD-ROM, Chapter 30, Section 4 **L1**

ASSESS/RETEACH

Monitor Progress

Assess students' completed graphic organizers using the Section Reading Support Transparency. Review the answers to the Guided Reading and Review worksheet.

Assess

Use the Section 4 Quiz to evaluate student understanding of key concepts in this section.

Reteach

Assign students the section summary in the Guide to the Essentials.

Targeted Resources

❏ Section Reading Support Transparencies **L1** **ELL**
❏ Guided Reading and Review booklet, p. 123 **L1**
❏ Section 4 Quiz, Units 9/10 booklet, p. 29 **L1** **L2**
❏ Guide to the Essentials, p. 154 **L1** **L2**
❏ Chapter Summary, Units 9/10 booklet, p. 25 **L1** **ELL**
❏ GoOnline: PHSchool.com, Chapter 30 Self-Test, Web Code: mra-9305
❏ Chapter 30 Tests, Units 9/10 booklet, pp. 30, 33

Homework _____

_____

Key
L1 Basic to Average   **L3** Average to Advanced
L2 For All Students   **ELL** English Language Learners

LESSON PLAN 31.1
The War Unfolds
⏰ *.5 Period, .25 Block*

Section Objectives

1. Learn about the events that led to the war between North Vietnam and South Vietnam.
2. Become familiar with the Vietnam policies of President Kennedy and Robert McNamara.
3. See how President Johnson changed the course of the war.

Vocabulary domino theory • Vietminh • Geneva Accords • Viet Cong • National Liberation Front • Gulf of Tonkin Resolution

Local Standards

FOCUS

Teach Key Concepts and Vocabulary
Ask students to explain how the United States became involved in Vietnam and how the American involvement deepened under Johnson.

Build Background Knowledge
Explain that America's Cold War containment policy called for the nation to resist the spread of communism into Vietnam.

Targeted Resources

❏ Activating Prior Knowledge, TE p. 1024 **L1**
❏ Color Transparencies, *Time Lines*, C8 **L2**
❏ Historical Outline Map Book, *War in Southeast Asia*, p. 70 **L1**
❏ Sounds of an Era Audio CD, *President John F. Kennedy*, 196 **L3**

INSTRUCT

Develop Understanding
Discuss why Eisenhower and Kennedy both chose to support the corrupt Diem regime in South Vietnam. What would have happened if they had withdrawn their support?

Monitor Comprehension
Ask students to describe the role of Robert McNamara in shaping American policy in Vietnam.

Targeted Resources

❏ Learning Styles Lesson Plans booklet, p. 64 **L2**
❏ Skills for Life booklet, p. 33 **L1**
❏ Presentation Pro CD-ROM, Chapter 31, Section 1 **L1**
❏ Prentice Hall U.S. History Video Collection, Vol. 20, *Post-War USA*

ASSESS/RETEACH

Monitor Progress
Assess students' completed graphic organizers using the Section Reading Support Transparency. Review the answers to the Guided Reading and Review worksheet.

Assess
Use the Section 1 Quiz to evaluate student understanding of key concepts in this section.

Reteach
Assign students the section summary in the Guide to the Essentials.

Targeted Resources

❏ Section Reading Support Transparencies **L1 ELL**
❏ Guided Reading and Review booklet, p. 124 **L1**
❏ Section 1 Quiz, Units 9/10 booklet, p. 37 **L1 L2**
❏ Guide to the Essentials, p. 156 **L1 L2**
❏ Social Studies Skills Tutor CD-ROM **L1**
❏ Guided Reading Audiotapes **ELL**
❏ Student Edition on Audio CD **ELL**

Homework _____

_____

Key
L1 Basic to Average   **L3** Average to Advanced
L2 For All Students   **ELL** English Language Learners

LESSON PLAN 31.2
Fighting the War
1 Period, .5 Block

Section Objectives

1. Learn how battlefield conditions in Vietnam affected American soldiers.
2. Be able to describe the course of the war between 1965 and 1968.
3. List reasons why the Tet Offensive was a turning point in the war.

Local Standards

Vocabulary land mine • saturation bombing • fragmentation bombs • Agent Orange • napalm • escalation • Ho Chi Minh Trail • hawks • doves • Tet Offensive

FOCUS

Teach Key Concepts and Vocabulary
Ask students to explain why the American armed forces, despite well-trained soldiers and superior equipment and supplies, had little success against the Viet Cong.

Build Background Knowledge
Explain that the Viet Cong were on familiar territory and that they fought in a manner—using guerrilla tactics—that frustrated the American forces.

Targeted Resources

❏ Activating Prior Knowledge, TE p. 1030 **L1**
❏ Color Transparencies, Historical Maps, A50 **L2**
❏ Sounds of an Era Audio CD, *Walter Cronkite, 1968* **L3**

INSTRUCT

Develop Understanding
Discuss the course of the war from 1965 to 1968, including Johnson's escalation and the Tet Offensive.

Monitor Comprehension
Ask students why the Tet Offensive was considered a turning point in the war.

Targeted Resources

❏ Learning with Documents booklet, *An Army Nurse Remembers*, p. 36 **L3**
❏ Biography, Literature, and Comparing Primary Sources booklet, *Experiences of a Young Soldier in Vietnam*, p. 83; *John McCain III*, p. 36 **L3**
❏ Presentation Pro CD-ROM, Chapter 31, Section 2 **L1**

ASSESS/RETEACH

Monitor Progress
Assess students' completed graphic organizers using the Section Reading Support Transparency. Review the answers to the Guided Reading and Review worksheet.

Assess
Use the Section 2 Quiz to evaluate student understanding of key concepts in this section.

Reteach
Assign students the section summary in the Guide to the Essentials.

Targeted Resources

❏ Section Reading Support Transparencies **L1 ELL**
❏ Guided Reading and Review booklet, p. 125 **L1**
❏ Section 2 Quiz, Units 9/10 booklet, p. 38 **L1 L2**
❏ Guide to the Essentials, p. 157 **L1**
❏ Guided Reading Audiotapes **ELL**
❏ Student Edition on Audio CD **ELL**

Homework _____
_____

Key
L1 Basic to Average   **L3** Average to Advanced
L2 For All Students   **ELL** English Language Learners

LESSON PLAN 31.3
Political Divisions
⏱ *1 Period, .5 Block*

Section Objectives

1. Find out about the role played by students in the protest movements of the 1960s.
2. Learn why President Johnson decided not to seek reelection.
3. Discover how the Vietnam War affected the election of 1968.

Local Standards

Vocabulary generation gap • New Left • teach-in • conscientious objector • deferment • Middle America

---

FOCUS

Teach Key Concepts and Vocabulary
Ask students to explain why, during the Vietnam era, students became activists in protest movements.

Build Background Knowledge
Explain to students that many young Americans, dissatisfied with their parents' values, attacked the institutions that reflected those values, including the educational establishment and the military.

Targeted Resources

❏ Activating Prior Knowledge, TE p. 1037 **L1**
❏ Sounds of an Era Audio CD, *President Johnson, 1968* **L3**

INSTRUCT

Develop Understanding
Discuss the various protest movements that arose during the 1960s, and connect the anti-war movements with the presidential election of 1968, including Johnson's decision not to run for another term.

Monitor Comprehension
Ask students what forms draft resistance took.

Targeted Resources

❏ Learning Styles Lesson Plans booklet, p. 65 **L2**
❏ Learning with Documents booklet, *The Port Huron Statement*, p. 95; *Antiwar Demonstrations*, 24 **L3**
❏ Presentation Pro CD-ROM, Chapter 31, Section 3 **L1**

ASSESS/RETEACH

Monitor Progress
Assess students' completed graphic organizers using the Section Reading Support Transparency. Review the answers to the Guided Reading and Review worksheet.

Assess
Use the Section 3 Quiz to evaluate student understanding of key concepts in this section.

Reteach
Assign students the section summary in the Guide to the Essentials.

Targeted Resources

❏ Section Reading Support Transparencies **L1** **ELL**
❏ Guided Reading and Review booklet, p. 126 **L1**
❏ Section 3 Quiz, Units 9/10 booklet, p. 39 **L1** **L2**
❏ Guide to the Essentials, p. 158 **L1** **L2**
❏ Guided Reading Audiotapes **ELL**
❏ Student Edition on Audio CD **ELL**

Homework _____

_____

Key
L1 Basic to Average   **L3** Average to Advanced
L2 For All Students   **ELL** English Language Learners

LESSON PLAN 31.4

The End of the War

⏰ *1 Period, .5 Block*

Section Objectives

1. Learn how President Nixon's policies led to American withdrawal from Vietnam.
2. Discover why President Nixon campaigned promising to restore law and order.
3. See what happened in Vietnam after the withdrawal of American forces.
4. Determine the legacy of the Vietnam War.

Vocabulary Paris peace talks • Vietnamization • silent majority • POW • MIA

Local Standards

FOCUS

Teach Key Concepts and Vocabulary
Ask students what finally brought the Vietnam War to a close.

Build Background Knowledge
Explain to students that antiwar protests continued throughout Nixon's first term, keeping pressure on the government to achieve a peace settlement.

Targeted Resources
❑ Activating Prior Knowledge, TE p. 1044 **L1**
❑ Color Transparencies, Historical Maps, A51 **L2**
❑ Sounds of an Era Audio CD, *John Kerry's "Winter Soldier" speech*, 1971 **L3**

INSTRUCT

Develop Understanding
Discuss Nixon's Vietnam policy and the interplay between military actions, such as the invasion of Cambodia, and the Paris peace talks.

Monitor Comprehension
Ask students why Nixon's escalation of the bombing and the invasion of Cambodia caused such outrage among opponents of the war.

Targeted Resources
❑ Biography, Literature, and Comparing Primary Sources booklet, *On the Tragedy of Kent State*, p. 157 **L3**
❑ Presentation Pro CD-ROM, Chapter 31, Section 4 **L1**
❑ Exploring Primary Sources in U.S. History CD-ROM, *The Vietnam Veterans Memorial,* **L3**

ASSESS/RETEACH

Monitor Progress
Assess students' completed graphic organizers using the Section Reading Support Transparency. Review the answers to the Guided Reading and Review worksheet.

Assess
Use the Section 4 Quiz to evaluate student understanding of key concepts in this section.

Reteach
Assign students the section summary in the Guide to the Essentials.

Targeted Resources
❑ Section Reading Support Transparencies **L1** **ELL**
❑ Guided Reading and Review booklet, p. 127 **L1**
❑ Section 4 Quiz, Units 9/10 booklet, p. 40 **L1** **L2**
❑ Guide to the Essentials, p. 159 **L1** **L2**
❑ GoOnline: PHSchool.com, Chapter 31 Self-Test, Web Code: mra-9315
❑ Chapter 31 Tests, Units 9/10 booklet, pp. 41, 44

Homework _____

Key
L1 Basic to Average **L3** Average to Advanced
L2 For All Students **ELL** English Language Learners

LESSON PLAN 32.1
Nixon's Domestic Policy
⏱ *1 Period, .5 Block*

Section Objectives

1. Find out how Richard Nixon's personality affected his relationship with his staff.
2. See how Nixon's domestic policies differed from those of his predecessors.
3. Learn how Nixon applied his "southern strategy" to the issue of civil rights and to the selection of Supreme Court justices.
4. Describe the first moon landing.

Vocabulary deficit spending • Organization of Petroleum Exporting Countries (OPEC) • embargo • New Federalism

Local Standards

FOCUS

Teach Key Concepts and Vocabulary
Ask students to explain how President Nixon's ideas about the proper size and role of the federal government differed from those of Kennedy and Johnson.

Build Background Knowledge
Explain to students that Republicans traditionally have tried to curb federal spending, whereas Democrats, starting with Franklin Roosevelt, have tended to support government spending to solve economic and social problems.

Targeted Resources
❏ Activating Prior Knowledge, TE p. 1058 **L1**
❏ Color Transparencies, Historical Maps, A57 **L2**

INSTRUCT

Develop Understanding
Discuss Nixon's domestic policy, including his approach to economic issues, social programs, and civil rights.

Monitor Comprehension
Ask students why Nixon went against his stated goals concerning federal spending and wage and price controls.

Targeted Resources
❏ Prentice Hall U.S. History Video Collection, Vol. 20, *Post-War USA*

ASSESS/RETEACH

Monitor Progress
Assess students' completed graphic organizers using the Section Reading Support Transparency.

Assess
Use the Section 1 Quiz to evaluate student understanding of key concepts in this section.

Reteach
Assign students the Guide to the Essentials.

Targeted Resources
❏ Section Reading Support Transparencies **L1 ELL**
❏ Guided Reading and Review booklet, p. 128 **L1**
❏ Section 1 Quiz, Units 9/10 booklet, p. 52 **L1 L2**
❏ Guide to the Essentials, p. 161 **L1 L2**

Homework _____

_____

Key
L1 Basic to Average   **L3** Average to Advanced
L2 For All Students   **ELL** English Language Learners

LESSON PLAN 32.2
Nixon's Foreign Policy
🕐 *1 Period, .5 Block*

Section Objectives

1. Learn about the role Henry Kissinger played in relaxing tensions between the United States and the major Communist powers.
2. Find out about Nixon's policy toward the People's Republic of China.
3. Discover how Nixon reached an agreement with the Soviet Union on limiting nuclear arms.

Vocabulary *realpolitik* • détente • SALT I

Local Standards

FOCUS

Teach Key Concepts and Vocabulary
Ask students to evaluate the success of Nixon's foreign policy.

Build Background Knowledge
Explain that Nixon had long been seen as a staunch anti-Communist, yet as President, he worked creatively with the Soviet Union and China to relax tensions.

Targeted Resources
- Activating Prior Knowledge, TE p. 1064 **L1**
- Color Transparencies, *Time Lines*, C9 **L2**
- Sounds of an Era Audio CD, *Nixon on the People's Republic of China, July 15, 1971* **L3**

INSTRUCT

Develop Understanding
Discuss with students how Nixon, the strong anti-Communist, managed to improve America's relationship with China and with the Soviet Union.

Monitor Comprehension
Ask students to describe the role Henry Kissinger played in shaping Nixon's foreign policy.

Targeted Resources
- Learning Styles Lesson Plans booklet, p. 66 **L2**
- Presentation Pro CD-ROM, Chapter 32, Section 2 **L1**
- American Heritage, My Brush With History, *A Cold War Test*, Student Edition pp. 1092–1093, Videotape

ASSESS/RETEACH

Monitor Progress
Assess students' completed graphic organizers using the Section Reading Support Transparency. Review the answers to the Guided Reading and Review worksheet.

Assess
Use the Section 2 Quiz to evaluate student understanding of key concepts in this section.

Reteach
Assign students the section summary in the Guide to the Essentials.

Targeted Resources
- Section Reading Support Transparencies **L1** **ELL**
- Guided Reading and Review booklet, p. 129 **L1**
- Section 2 Quiz, Units 9/10 booklet, p. 53 **L1** **L2**
- Guide to the Essentials, p. 162 **L1** **L2**
- Guided Reading Audiotapes **ELL**
- Student Edition on Audio CD **ELL**

Homework _____

_____

Key
L1 Basic to Average **L3** Average to Advanced
L2 For All Students **ELL** English Language Learners

LESSON PLAN 32.3

The Watergate Scandal

🕐 *1 Period, .5 Block*

Section Objectives	Local Standards

Section Objectives

1. See how the Nixon White House battled its political enemies.
2. Find out how the Committee to Reelect the President conducted itself during Nixon's reelection campaign.
3. Learn about the Watergate break-in, and see how the story of the scandal unfolded.
4. Discover the events that led directly to Nixon's resignation.

Vocabulary wiretap • Watergate scandal • special prosecutor • impeach

FOCUS

Teach Key Concepts and Vocabulary
Ask students to explain why Nixon decided to resign the presidency.

Build Background Knowledge
Remind students that Nixon had committed at least one impeachable offense—covering up the Watergate break-in—and that the House's impeachment mechanism had been put in motion by the time of his resignation.

Targeted Resources
❏ Activating Prior Knowledge, TE p. 1070 **L1**
❏ Color Transparencies, *Political Cartoons*, B18 **L2**
❏ Sounds of an Era Audio CD, *Nixon's Watergate Speeches* **L3**

INSTRUCT

Develop Understanding
Discuss Nixon's questionable actions while President, such as keeping an "enemies list" and harassing opponents. Ask students whether or not these actions constituted abuse of power—one of the charges made by the House Judiciary Committee.

Monitor Comprehension
Ask students how the atmosphere in the White House might have encouraged the Watergate scandal.

Targeted Resources
❏ Skills for Life booklet, p. 34 **L1**
❏ Biography, Literature, and Comparing Primary Sources booklet, *Unraveling the Story of Watergate*, p. 85; *On Nixon's Impeachment*, p. 159 **L3**
❏ Presentation Pro CD-ROM, Chapter 32, Section 3 **L1**
❏ Exploring Primary Sources in U.S. History CD-ROM, *Bugging at the Watergate* **L3**

ASSESS/RETEACH

Monitor Progress
Assess students' completed graphic organizers using the Section Reading Support Transparency.

Assess
Use the Section 3 Quiz to evaluate student understanding of key concepts in this section.

Reteach
Assign students the Guide to the Essentials.

Homework _____

_____

Targeted Resources
❏ Section Reading Support Transparencies **L1 ELL**
❏ Guided Reading and Review booklet, p. 130 **L1**
❏ Section 3 Quiz, Units 9/10 booklet, p. 54 **L1 L2**
❏ Guide to the Essentials, p. 163 **L1 L2**

Key
L1 Basic to Average **L3** Average to Advanced
L2 For All Students **ELL** English Language Learners

LESSON PLAN 32.4
The Ford Administration
⏱ .5 Period, .25 Block

Section Objectives

1. Find out how Gerald Ford became President, and learn why he pardoned Richard Nixon.
2. See the types of economic problems the Ford administration faced.
3. Learn about the foreign policy actions Ford took.
4. See how Americans celebrated the nation's bicentennial.

Local Standards

Vocabulary stagflation • War Powers Act • Helsinki Accords • bicentennial

FOCUS	Targeted Resources

Teach Key Concepts and Vocabulary
Ask students to list the problems President Ford faced upon taking office in 1974.

Build Background Knowledge
Explain to students that Ford was a popular politician with a strong congressional record, but he had limited experience as an administrator or in foreign affairs.

❏ Activating Prior Knowledge, TE p. 1078 **L1**

INSTRUCT	Targeted Resources

Develop Understanding
Discuss with students how Ford dealt with the main issues of the day, including the Nixon pardon, the stalled economy, and the collapse of South Vietnam.

Monitor Comprehension
Ask students why the WIN program failed.

❏ Skills for Life booklet, p. 34 **L1**

❏ Biography, Literature, and Comparing Primary Sources booklet, *Unraveling the Story of Watergate*, p. 85; *On Nixon's Impeachment*, p. 159 **L3**

❏ Presentation Pro CD-ROM, Chapter 32, Section 3 **L1**

❏ Exploring Primary Sources in U.S. History CD-ROM, *Bugging at the Watergate* **L3**

ASSESS/RETEACH	Targeted Resources

Monitor Progress
Assess students' completed graphic organizers using the Section Reading Support Transparency. Review the answers to the Guided Reading and Review worksheet.

Assess
Use the Section 4 Quiz to evaluate student understanding of key concepts in this section.

Reteach
Assign students the section summary in the Guide to the Essentials.

❏ Section Reading Support Transparency **L1** **ELL**

❏ Guided Reading and Review booklet, p. 39 **L1**

❏ Section 3 Quiz, Unit 9/10 booklet, p. 28 **L1** **L2**

❏ Guide to the Essentials, p. 49 **L1** **L2**

❏ Social Studies Skills Tutor CD-ROM **L1**

❏ Guided Reading Audiotapes **ELL**

❏ Student Edition on Audio CD **ELL**

Homework _____
_____

Key
L1 Basic to Average   **L3** Average to Advanced
L2 For All Students   **ELL** English Language Learners

LESSON PLAN 32.5

The Carter Administration

🕐 *1 Period, .5 Block*

Section Objectives

1. Discover some changes Jimmy Carter brought to the presidency.
2. Learn how Carter dealt with domestic issues.
3. Find out about the ideals that guided Carter's foreign policy.
4. Discover some factors that influenced the outcome of the 1980 election.

Local Standards

Vocabulary incumbent • deregulation • amnesty • affirmative action • Camp David Accords • dissident

---

FOCUS

Teach Key Concepts and Vocabulary
Ask students to link the beliefs that President Carter outlined in his Inaugural Address to policies he later pursued—in the areas of civil rights and diplomacy.

Build Background Knowledge
Explain that in the post-Watergate era being an outsider gave Carter an advantage in getting elected but a disadvantage in promoting his policies in Congress.

Targeted Resources

❏ Activating Prior Knowledge, TE p. 1083 **L1**
❏ Color Transparencies, *The Way It Works*, H20 **L2**
❏ Sounds of an Era Audio CD, *Carter on Hostages in Iran* **L3**

INSTRUCT

Develop Understanding
Discuss why Carter's outsider status and his choice of other outsiders as his key advisors hampered his ability to work with Congress.

Monitor Comprehension
Ask students to identify the Carter administration's foreign policy successes and failures.

Targeted Resources

❏ Learning Styles Lesson Plans booklet, p. 67 **L2**
❏ Learning with Documents booklet, *Barbara Jordan, Keynote Address to the Democratic National Convention*, p. 96 **L3**
❏ Biography, Literature, and Comparing Primary Sources booklet, *Patricia Roberts Harris*, p. 37 **L3**

ASSESS/RETEACH

Monitor Progress
Assess students' completed graphic organizers using the Section Reading Support Transparency.

Assess
Use the Section 5 Quiz to evaluate student understanding of key concepts in this section.

Reteach
Assign students the section summary in the Guide to the Essentials.

Targeted Resources

❏ Section Reading Support Transparencies **L1** **ELL**
❏ Guided Reading and Review, p. 132 **L1**
❏ Section 5 Quiz, Units 9/10 booklet, p. 56 **L1**
❏ Guide to the Essentials, p. 165 **L1** **L2**
❏ GoOnline: PHSchool.com, Chapter 32 Self-Test, Web Code: mra-0326
❏ Chapter 32 Tests, Units 9/10 booklet, pp. 57, 60

Homework _____

_____

Key
L1 Basic to Average   **L3** Average to Advanced
L2 For All Students   **ELL** English Language Learners

LESSON PLAN 33.1

Roots of the New Conservatism

⏱ *.5 Period, .25 Block*

Section Objectives

1. Find out about the major events in Ronald Reagan's political career.
2. Learn how conservatism evolved in the years between the 1930s and the 1970s.
3. Discover why the 1980 election marked a turning point in United States history.

Vocabulary Reagan Democrat • New Right • televangelism

Local Standards

FOCUS

Teach Key Concepts and Vocabulary
Ask students to list the aspects of government and society that the conservatives opposed.

Build Background Knowledge
Explain to students that the modern conservative movement arose in response to the continued growth of the federal government, starting with the New Deal.

Targeted Resources

❏ Activating Prior Knowledge, TE p. 1096 **L1**
❏ Color Transparencies, *American Photo*, F10; *American Diversity*, G13, G14 **L2**
❏ Sounds of an Era Audio CD, *Barry Goldwater, 1964; Ronald Reagan* **L3**

INSTRUCT

Develop Understanding
Have students describe the aims of the various government programs that conservatives opposed. Discuss whether conservatives argued with the aims, the methods, or both.

Monitor Comprehension
Have students identify the social issues that brought the New Right together.

Targeted Resources

❏ Learning Styles Lesson Plans booklet, p. 68 **L2**
❏ Skills for Life booklet, p. 35 **L1**
❏ Learning with Documents booklet, *Speaking for the President*, p. 38 **L3**
❏ Presentation Pro CD-ROM, Chapter 33, Section 1 **L1**
❏ Prentice Hall U.S. History Video Collection, Vol. 20, Post-War USA

ASSESS/RETEACH

Monitor Progress
Assess students' completed graphic organizers using the Section Reading Support Transparency. Review the answers to the Guided Reading and Review worksheet.

Assess
Use the Section 1 Quiz to evaluate student understanding of key concepts in this section.

Reteach
Assign students the section summary in the Guide to the Essentials.

Targeted Resources

❏ Section Reading Support Transparencies **L1 ELL**
❏ Guided Reading and Review booklet, p. 133 **L1**
❏ Section 1 Quiz, Units 9/10 booklet, p. 64 **L1 L2**
❏ Guide to the Essentials, p. 167 **L1 L2**
❏ Social Studies Skills Tutor CD-ROM **L1**
❏ Guided Reading Audiotapes **ELL**
❏ Student Edition on Audio CD **ELL**

Homework _____
_____

Key
L1 Basic to Average   **L3** Average to Advanced
L2 For All Students   **ELL** English Language Learners

LESSON PLAN 33.2
The Reagan Revolution
⏱ *1 Period, .5 Block*

Section Objectives

1. Read to find out how President Reagan attempted to change the economy.
2. Find out how Reagan changed the federal government.
3. Reflect on major initiatives and key foreign policy crises of Reagan's first term.
4. Explore the ways in which the economy moved from recession to recovery in the early 1980s.

Local Standards

Vocabulary supply-side economics • New Federalism • Strategic Defense Initiative (SDI)

FOCUS

Teach Key Concepts and Vocabulary
Ask students to identify the changes Reagan made in the economy and government.
Build Background Knowledge
Remind students that Reagan won the presidency in a landslide, and he used his mandate to make revolutionary changes based on conservative principles.

Targeted Resources
❑ Activating Prior Knowledge, TE p. 1102 **L1**
❑ Sounds of an Era Audio CD, *Ronald Reagan, 1981* **L3**

INSTRUCT

Develop Understanding
Discuss Reagan's program for change, including supply-side economics, tax cuts, limits on government, and military buildup.
Monitor Comprehension
Ask students how Reagan's foreign policy fit in with his goal of restoring the country's strength.

Targeted Resources
❑ Learning with Documents booklet, *Ronald Reagan, "These Are the Boys of Pointe du Hoc,"* p. 97 **L3**
❑ Presentation Pro CD-ROM, Chapter 33, Section 2 **L1**
❑ Exploring Primary Sources in U.S. History CD-ROM, *A Time for Choosing, Ronald Reagan* **L3**

ASSESS/RETEACH

Monitor Progress
Assess students' completed graphic organizers using the Section Reading Support Transparency. Review the answers to the Guided Reading and Review worksheet.
Assess
Use the Section 2 Quiz to evaluate student understanding of key concepts in this section.
Reteach
Assign students the section summary in the Guide to the Essentials.

Targeted Resources
❑ Section Reading Support Transparencies **L1** **ELL**
❑ Guided Reading and Review booklet, p. 134 **L1**
❑ Section 2 Quiz, Units 9/10 booklet, p. 65 **L1** **L2**
❑ Guide to the Essentials, p. 168 **L1** **L2**
❑ Guided Reading Audiotapes **ELL**
❑ Student Edition on Audio CD **ELL**

Homework _____

_____

Key
L1 Basic to Average   **L3** Average to Advanced
L2 For All Students   **ELL** English Language Learners

LESSON PLAN 33.3

Reagan's Second Term

🕐 *1 Period, .5 Block*

Section Objectives	**Local Standards**

Section Objectives

1. Observe the ways in which the United States experienced a renewal of patriotism in the 1980s.
2. Find out about some important social debates that continued through Reagan's term in office.
3. See how the economy evolved during the 1980s.
4. Discover how Reagan's hands-off style of governing led to problems.
5. Consider the legacy of Reagan's presidency.

Vocabulary AIDS • Sandinista • Contra • Iran-Contra affair • INF Treaty • entitlement

FOCUS	**Targeted Resources**
Teach Key Concepts and Vocabulary Ask students to identify problems that arose during Reagan's second term. **Build Background Knowledge** Explain that Reagan made Americans feel proud and optimistic, despite ongoing concerns.	❏ Activating Prior Knowledge, TE p. 1108 **L1** ❏ Sounds of an Era Audio CD, *Ronald Reagan, 1984* **L3**

INSTRUCT	**Targeted Resources**
Develop Understanding Discuss the domestic and foreign issues that developed during Reagan's second term. **Monitor Comprehension** Ask students how Soviet-American relations changed during Reagan's presidency.	❏ Learning with Documents booklet, *Short-Lived Approval*, p. 72 **L3** ❏ Biography, Literature, and Comparing Primary Sources booklet, *On the Legacy of the Civil Rights Movement*, p. 161; *Masters of the Universe*, p. 88 **L3** ❏ Presentation Pro CD-ROM, Chapter 33, Section 3 **L1**

ASSESS/RETEACH	**Targeted Resources**
Monitor Progress Assess students' completed graphic organizers using the Section Reading Support Transparency. Review the answers to the Guided Reading and Review worksheet. **Assess** Use the Section 3 Quiz to evaluate student understanding of key concepts in this section. **Reteach** Assign students the section summary in the Guide to the Essentials.	❏ Section Reading Support Transparencies **L1** **ELL** ❏ Guided Reading and Review booklet, p. 135 **L1** ❏ Section 3 Quiz, Units 9/10 booklet, p. 66 **L1** **L2** ❏ Guide to the Essentials, p. 169 **L1** **L2** ❏ Guided Reading Audiotapes **ELL** ❏ Student Edition on Audio CD **ELL**

Homework _____

_____

Key
L1 Basic to Average   **L3** Average to Advanced
L2 For All Students   **ELL** English Language Learners

LESSON PLAN 33.4

The George H. W. Bush Presidency

🕐 *1 Period, .5 Block*

Section Objectives

1. See what challenges George H. W. Bush faced in the 1988 presidential election.
2. Find out how the Cold War came to an end.
3. Learn about the ways in which the United States played a new international role after the Cold War.
4. Observe the effect domestic issues had on Bush's presidency.

Vocabulary Strategic Arms Reduction Treaty • Persian Gulf War • downsizing

Local Standards

FOCUS

Teach Key Concepts and Vocabulary
Ask students to identify Bush's major triumphs in foreign affairs.

Build Background Knowledge
Remind students that the United States had geared its foreign policy for many years toward a Cold War with the Soviet Union.

Targeted Resources
- ❏ Activating Prior Knowledge, TE p. 1114 **L1**
- ❏ Sounds of an Era Audio CD, *George Bush, 1990* **L3**

INSTRUCT

Develop Understanding
Discuss the end of the Cold War and the resulting changes in the role of the United States internationally.

Monitor Comprehension
Ask students to explain how the Persian Gulf War started and how the United States won.

Targeted Resources
- ❏ Learning Styles Lesson Plans booklet, p. 69 **L2**
- ❏ Biography, Literature, and Comparing Primary Sources booklet, *Melissa Rathbun-Nealy*, p. 38 **L3**
- ❏ Presentation Pro CD-ROM, Chapter 33, Section 4 **L1**

ASSESS/RETEACH

Monitor Progress
Assess students' completed graphic organizers using the Section Reading Support Transparency. Review the answers to the Guided Reading and Review worksheet.

Assess
Use the Section 4 Quiz to evaluate student understanding of key concepts in this section.

Reteach
Assign students the section summary in the Guide to the Essentials.

Targeted Resources
- ❏ Section Reading Support Transparencies **L1 ELL**
- ❏ Guided Reading and Review booklet, p. 136 **L1**
- ❏ Section 4 Quiz, Units 9/10 booklet, p. 67 **L1 L2**
- ❏ Guide to the Essentials, p. 170 **L1 L2**
- ❏ Chapter Summary, Units 9/10 booklet, p. 63 **L1 ELL**
- ❏ GoOnline: PHSchool.com, Chapter 33 Self-Test, Web Code: mra-0335
- ❏ Chapter 33 Tests, Units 9/10 booklet, pp. 68, 71

Homework _____

_____

Key
L1 Basic to Average **L3** Average to Advanced
L2 For All Students **ELL** English Language Learners

LESSON PLAN 34.1
Politics in Recent Years

.5 Period, .25 Block

Section Objectives

| | Local Standards |

1. Find out what led to Bill Clinton's election in 1992 and what issues he tackled in his first term.
2. See why Republicans issued a Contract with America.
3. Read about the scandals that were debated during Clinton's second term.
4. Think about the results of the 2000 election and the goals the new President set.

Vocabulary Contract with America • Whitewater affair

FOCUS

Teach Key Concepts and Vocabulary
Ask students to explain how Clinton, a "New Democrat," got elected in 1992.

Build Background Knowledge
Remind students that economic issues dominated the campaign.

Targeted Resources

❏ Activating Prior Knowledge, TE p. 1126 **L1**
❏ Color Transparencies, *Historical Maps*, A52, A54 **L2**
❏ Sounds of an Era Audio CD, *Bill Clinton's Democratic Nomination Acceptance Speech*, 1992; *Anti–National Health Care Television Ad*; *President Clinton on Monica Lewinsky Scandal; Al Gore's Concession Speech*, 2000; *George W. Bush Inauguration Speech* **L3**

INSTRUCT

Develop Understanding
Discuss how Clinton approached important economic and social issues as President.

Monitor Comprehension
Ask students how Republicans gained a majority in both houses of Congress in 1994, and what effects this shift of power had.

Targeted Resources

❏ Learning with Documents booklet, Campaign Strategies '96, p. 73; *William J. Clinton's Final State of the Union Address*, p. 98 **L3**
❏ Biography, Literature, and Comparing Primary Sources booklet, *The Republican Revolution*, p. 89 **L3**
❏ Exploring Primary Sources in U.S. History CD-ROM, *On the Pulse of Morning, Maya Angelou; Inaugural Address, President George W. Bush* **L3**

ASSESS/RETEACH

Monitor Progress
Assess students' completed graphic organizers using the Section Reading Support Transparency.

Assess
Use the Section 1 Quiz to evaluate student understanding of key concepts in this section.

Reteach
Assign students the Guide to the Essentials.

Targeted Resources

❏ Section Reading Support Transparencies **L1** **ELL**
❏ Guided Reading and Review booklet, p. 137 **L1**
❏ Section 1 Quiz, Units 9/10 booklet, p. 75 **L1** **L2**
❏ Guide to the Essentials, p. 174 **L1** **L2**

Homework _____

_____

Key
L1 Basic to Average   **L3** Average to Advanced
L2 For All Students   **ELL** English Language Learners

LESSON PLAN 34.2

The United States in a New World

🕐 *1 Period, .5 Block*

Section Objectives

1. Read about political changes that took place in the post–Cold War world.
2. Read about the conflicts that proved difficult to resolve during the post–Cold War world.
3. Describe the American reaction to the terrorist attacks of September 11, 2001.

Vocabulary proliferation • apartheid • economic sanctions

Local Standards

FOCUS	**Targeted Resources**

Teach Key Concepts and Vocabulary
Ask students to explain how the post–Cold War world offered both hope for the future and new challenges.

Build Background Knowledge
Remind students that the United States now stood as the world's lone superpower.

- ❏ Activating Prior Knowledge, TE p. 1133 **L1**
- ❏ Color Transparencies, *American Diversity*, G15 **L2**
- ❏ Historical Outline Map Book, *The World*, p. 71; *Western Hemisphere*, p. 72; *Africa*, p. 74; *Asia*, p. 75; *East Asia*, p. 76; *Europe*, p. 77; *The Middle East*, p. 78; *North America*, p. 79 **L1**

INSTRUCT	**Targeted Resources**

Develop Understanding
Discuss the issues and conflicts that beset the post–Cold War world, and have students examine the role and responsibility of the United States in this new world.

Monitor Comprehension
Ask students to explain why the United States invaded Iraq in 2003.

- ❏ Learning Styles Lesson Plans booklet, p. 70 **L2**
- ❏ Presentation Pro CD-ROM, Chapter 34, Section 2 **L1**

ASSESS/RETEACH	**Targeted Resources**

Monitor Progress
Assess students' completed graphic organizers using the Section Reading Support Transparency. Review the answers to the Guided Reading and Review worksheet.

Assess
Use the Section 2 Quiz to evaluate student understanding of key concepts in this section.

Reteach
Assign students the section summary in the Guide to the Essentials.

- ❏ Section Reading Support Transparencies **L1** **ELL**
- ❏ Guided Reading and Review booklet, p. 138 **L1**
- ❏ Section 2 Quiz, Units 9/10 booklet, p. 76 **L1** **L2**
- ❏ Guide to the Essentials, p. 175 **L1** **L2**
- ❏ Guided Reading Audiotape **ELL**
- ❏ Student Edition on Audio CD **ELL**

Homework _____

_____

Key
L1 Basic to Average   **L3** Average to Advanced
L2 For All Students   **ELL** English Language Learners

LESSON PLAN 34.3

Americans in the New Millenium

⏱ *1 Period, .5 Block*

Section Objectives

1. Learn about the factors that contributed to the growing diversity of the nation's population.
2. Find out how Americans disagreed about how to make diversity work.
3. Read to find out how the technological revolution at the end of the twentieth century affected American life.
4. Discover the impact of the expanding global economy.

Local Standards

Vocabulary bilingual education • Internet • North American Free Trade Agreement (NAFTA) • World Trade Organization (WTO) • multinational corporation

FOCUS

Teach Key Concepts and Vocabulary
Ask students to describe the challenges that new waves of immigration and an aging population pose for the United States.

Build Background Knowledge
Remind students that the United States is a land of immigrants, but immigration has often been a subject of fierce debate.

Targeted Resources

❏ Activating Prior Knowledge, TE p. 1142 **L1**
❏ Color Transparencies, *American Diversity,* G12; Historical Maps, A53, A59; *Fine Art,* E19, E20; *Political Cartoons,* B19, B20; *Time Lines,* C10 **L2**
❏ Historical Outline Map Book, *Western Hemisphere,* p. 72; *North America,* p. 79; *Political United States,* p. 82 **L1**

INSTRUCT

Develop Understanding
Discuss the challenges facing the country, including demographic changes, the technological revolution, and the global economy.

Monitor Comprehension
Ask students to explain why nations make trade agreements such as NAFTA.

Targeted Resources

❏ Learning with Documents booklet, *Trying to Break the Cycle of Crime,* p. 39 **L3**
❏ Biography, Literature, and Comparing Primary Sources booklet, *Ron Brown,* p. 39; *On Immigration Policy,* p. 163 **L3**
❏ Exploring Primary Sources in U.S. History CD-ROM, *Texas State Constitution* **L3**

ASSESS/RETEACH

Monitor Progress
Assess students' completed graphic organizers using the Section Reading Support Transparency.

Assess
Use the Section 3 Quiz to evaluate student understanding of key concepts in this section.

Reteach
Assign students the Guide to the Essentials.

Targeted Resources

❏ Section Reading Support Transparencies **L1** **ELL**
❏ Guided Reading and Review, p. 139 **L1**
❏ Section 3 Quiz, Units 9/10 booklet, p. 77 **L1** **L2**
❏ Guide to the Essentials, p. 176 **L1** **L2**
❏ GoOnline: PHSchool.com, Chapter 34 Self-Test, Web Code: mra-0344
❏ Chapter 34 Tests, Units 9/10 booklet, pp. 78, 81

Homework _____

_____

Key
L1 Basic to Average   **L3** Average to Advanced
L2 For All Students   **ELL** English Language Learners